The Question of

Freemasonry

and the

Founding Fathers

Was America Founded by Freemasons?

David Barton

Aledo, Texas
www.wallbuilders.com

Additional materials available from:
WallBuilders
P.O. Box 397
Aledo, TX 76008
(817) 441-6044
www.wallbuilders.com

Cover Painting:
Used courtesy of the Supreme Council, 33°, Southern Jurisdiction, U. S. A., Washington, D. C.

Cover Design:
Jeremiah Pent
Lincoln-Jackson
838 Walden Way
Franklin, TN 37064

Library of Congress Cataloging-in-Publication Data
366
Barton, David.
The question of freemasonry and the founding fathers
Aledo, TX: WallBuilder Press
136 p.; 21 cm.
Endnotes included.
ISBN 10: 1-932225-37-4
ISBN 13: 978-1-932225-37-2
1. Freemasonry.   2. Founding Fathers.   3. Religion.   I. Title.

Printed in the United States of America

Table of Contents

CHAPTER I

Overview

Although hundreds of books have been written on the subject of American Freemasonry, this one examines an aspect rarely touched: did Freemasonry substantially impact the American Founding? This question will be examined from a Christian perspective, illuminating not only historical occurrences but also Biblical considerations.

While few Americans concern themselves with whether Freemasonry had an impact in the Founding Era, it is nevertheless an important question – especially for Christians. The answer directly impacts the broader issue of whether America was founded on, or against, Judeo-Christian principles.

The question in this book is actually the result of merging three otherwise separate and independent subjects of academic inquiries among Christian writers. Those three areas include:

CHRISTIAN EXPOSÉS OF MODERN FREEMASONRY. Christians who have studied modern American Freemasonry in a serious manner have documented irrefutably that it is antithetical, hostile, and heretical to many orthodox Christian and Biblical teachings. In fact, part of the attention focused on this subject has been the result of high-ranking Masonic officials who – following their personal conversion to Christ – renounced their Masonic membership and then wrote exposés about the untenable spiritual heresies permeating Masonic teachings. [1]

FREEMASONRY IN THE LIVES OF THE FOUNDING FATHERS. Numerous current works declare that the overwhelming majority of America's Founding Fathers were active members in and leaders of the secret society of Freemasonry. As the Founders designed America's governing documents, its governmental seals and symbols, and its capital city, they incorporated Masonic beliefs and symbols throughout. America is therefore supposedly erected on the foundation of Freemasonry. [2]

THE INFLUENCE OF CHRISTIANITY IN THE AMERICAN FOUNDING. For more than two centuries, distinguished educators, statesmen, presidents, congresses, judges, and courts have declared that America was founded as a Christian nation. [3] Numerous works – both early and modern – have substantiated this declaration. [4]

If the first two points are correct, then logically, the third must be incorrect. That is, if American Freemasonry is unChristian, and if the vast majority of those who framed our documents were members of this heretical organization, then America could not have been founded as a Christian nation. Furthermore, if the foundations on which the nation was built are ignoble and polluted, then God could no more bless America than He could ancient nations consecrated to BAAL, DAGON, or MOLECH, or modern nations dedicated to secularism, relativism, statism, hedonism, or materialism. After all, the promise of Scripture is clear and unambiguous: "Blessed is that nation whose God is the Lord" [PSALM 33:12]; there exists no stronger basis for the blessing of the Almighty upon a nation.

Seemingly countless modern Christian books and websites – convinced that the first two points are correct, and that there was a widespread Masonic influence in the American Founding – disparage and attack any suggestion that America was, or is, a Christian nation. Their assaults have affected many American Christians, who – becoming disappointed about their county – lose their sense of patriotism and refuse to become involved in civic or political affairs. They see no enduring hope for a nation that they believe was formed on a pagan foundation. Yet, their conclusion – while sincerely believed – is entirely mistaken, for it can be indisputably shown that one of their key suppositions is completely erroneous.

This work will address the issue of American Freemasonry in the Founding Era, and therefore clarify whether America can be considered as having Biblical foundations. The plumbline for truth in this investigation will not be the cacophony of modern voices and writings; rather, it will be original documents from the Founding Era. [†] Before the inquiry begins, it is important to understand more about the organization at the center of this investigation.

Most of today's citizens know little about American Freemasonry beyond the fact that it is a fraternal group involved in charitable endeavors. For example, the branch of Freemasonry called the Scottish Rite is famous for its Shrine Burn Centers, Crippled Children's Hospitals, and Scottish Rite Learning Centers that work with dyslexic students. Within the Scottish Rite are Masons called "Shriners" (easily recognizable in public settings because of their red fez hats), often seen driving midget cars in parades; standing at street intersections, walking amidst traffic, collecting donations; or working with students in the D.A.R.E. anti-drug programs. Yet this charitable image is only a tiny part of Freemasonry.

SHRINERS IN A PARADE

American Freemasonry is a massive organization with a meticulous and rigidly organized infrastructure, having a complete system of degree rituals as well as religious and philosophical teachings. Freemasonry exists as America's largest and oldest secret society, [††] tracing its

---

[†] The Author has one of America's largest private libraries focused on the American Founding, with some 100,000 documents – either originals, or copies of originals – that pre-date 1812. Additionally, the library contains thousands of documents from the post-1812 period. It is to these documents that the Author turns in the investigation of the issues addressed in this book.

[††] Other American secret societies include the Independent Order of Odd Fellows (I.O.O.F), Order of Elks, Order of Skull and Bones, Ku Klux Klan, National Grange, Woodmen of the World, the Carbonari, Knights of Pythias, etc.

American origins to around 1730 in Pennsylvania and Massachusetts. [5] Two-and-a-half centuries later, in 1959, it reached its peak membership, with over four million men [†] as members. [6]

Masons are frequently the prominent and visible members of a community, often including its elected officials, leading businessmen, attorneys, educators, judges, law-enforcement officers. Because of the disproportionately high percentage of high-ranking and powerful officials in such a relatively small but secret organization, conspiracy theories have long abounded about its influence (e.g., that Masonry works with the Mafia; is affiliated with the Illuminati; controls and directs the New World Order; etc.). And Masonry is often charged with preferentialism; it is true – and even logical – that Masons prefer other Masons in employment, promotion, and appointment to offices (just as Christians, atheists, Boy Scouts, or whomever would also prefer their own).

Freemasonry today is in a downward membership spiral, with only half the numbers of just a few decades ago, and with most of the remaining members being inactive. Although there are still 26,500 lodges nationwide, [7] many are under-populated and relatively inactive.

Although Masonic members include many political officials, Masonry does not involve itself directly in politics. Nevertheless, there are two political positions to which it unswervingly holds: (1) separation of church and state (but not in the original historical sense as intended by the framers of the Constitution, but rather in its more modern and secular judicial sense that limits many public religious expressions); and (2) the replacement of religiously-affiliated schools with secular public schools.

Finally, Masonry includes a very religious component, that is highly universalist and deistic. The god recognized by Masonry is

---

† Officially, women are not permitted to become members of Masonic Lodges. While there are a handful of Lodges that describe themselves as Co-Masonic, admitting both men and women, they are not recognized by Masonry as official Lodges. Masonry does have numerous auxiliary organizations for Masonic relatives, including Order of Eastern Star (for female relatives of Masons), the Order of DeMolay (for boys aged 12–21), Job's Daughters (for girls aged 10-20) and the International Order of the Rainbow for Girls (for girls 11–20).

whatever god any individual Mason might recognize, [†] whether the Judeo-Christian God or a pagan or pantheistic god. To avoid religious controversy, all deities are recognized in Masonry by a single deistic name: G.A.O.T.U. (the **G**reat **A**rchitect **O**f **T**he **U**niverse).

This is a brief summary of the public and more visible side of modern Freemasonry, but since it is a secret society, there obviously is much that most citizens today never see or know. Yet, for any studious individual, there is very little about Masonry that is any longer completely secret. Over its three centuries, so many Masons have left their Lodges and written exposés that there are no genuine secrets left about Freemasonry. And even though Masons have oral rather than written rituals (as well as a system of secret signals, handshakes, and symbols) in order to preserve their secrets, those "secrets" have already been made public by the many exposés. As one source accurately observes: "Many Masons say that [Masonry] is more accurately described as a 'society with secrets.' . . . [for] most Masons are completely public with their affiliation, Masonic buildings are usually clearly marked, and meeting times are generally a matter of public record." [8]

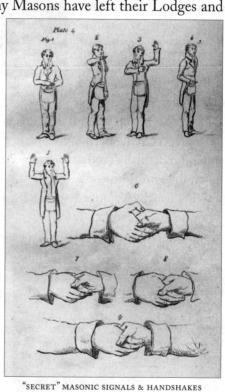

"SECRET" MASONIC SIGNALS & HANDSHAKES

In a historical sense, American Freemasonry has a colorful – and checkered – past, tracing its roots to Europe.

[†] Atheists are not permitted to be Masons; a Freemason must acknowledge a god of some type – a god to be defined by each individual Mason.

Originally, masons were the craftsmen who traveled across Europe more than a thousand years ago building the cathedrals, abbeys, churches, castles, and other stone buildings. These masons who journeyed the continent (and who actually did the physical stone-cutting and stone-laying) were often members of masons' lodges. (A useful analogy would be to consider those early masonic lodges as precursors of today's union halls.) The traveling masons were called free masons – a

NOTRE DAME CATHEDRAL, THE COLISEUM, AND OTHER
STONE STRUCTURES WERE BUILT BY MASONS

skilled mason who worked for himself and who was thus "free" to travel the land practicing his trade. [9] The free masons devised a system of secret signs and handshakes that identified them to other free masons (serving much the same purpose as would today's union card). The non-traveling masons usually belonged to local masonic guilds rather than lodges. They lived and worked in one area, ready to do local construction jobs or repairs; and these local masons were often employed by the traveling free masons for their construction projects. [10]

EARLY MASONS AT WORK

Early masons had three degrees, based on the experience of the worker. (Interestingly, the same three levels are still found in many unions today.) Novices who entered the craft to learn the trade of stonecutting were called "Entered Apprentices." After several years of apprentice work, they became "Fellowcrafts." Upon finally mastering the trade, they were called "Master Masons."

This type of artisan masonry represents the age known as "operative masonry" – the age when those who were masons actually had architectural skills and operated as literal stone masons. [†] During this operative era, the conduct of Freemasons as members of masonic guilds was originally governed by the Old York [††] Constitutions of 926 A. D., and then by Old Charges of 938 A. D. These early masonic regulations gave "charges" to the mason in four areas: (1) God and religion (very important not only because a primary source of their work was cathedrals but also because most nations had state-established religions); (2) masonry as a professional craft (regulations regarding the conduct, behavior, and training of masons); (3) the science of geometry (understanding the scientific and mathematical basis for architectural designs and calculations); and (4) regal duty (instruction in royal protocol since

EARLY MASONIC CHARGES FROM 1400 A.D. (LEFT) AND 1701 A.D. (RIGHT) NOTICE THAT THE 1701 CONSTITUTIONS BEGIN WITH THE DECLARATON: "THE MIGHT OF THE FATHER OF HEAVEN, WITH THE WISDOM OF HIS GLORIOUS SON, THROUGH THE GRACE AND GOODNESS OF THE HOLY GHOST, THREE PERSONS IN ONE GODHEAD."

[†] Today's Freemasonry – which claims to be the descendant of operative masonry – is called "speculative masonry" and will be discussed in detail in this and a later chapter. Contrary to the claims of today's Freemasonry, there is very little similarity between speculative masonry and operative masonry; probably 99 percent of today's Freemasons have no idea whatsoever of how to construct a stone building. Nevertheless, it is important to know the current claims in order better to understand the heresies in the modern organization.

[††] York is a town in England that was the governing center for the lodges of operative masons.

much of what was being built was at the request of monarchs, nobles, and governmental church officials).

In the area regarding God and religion, the 926 A. D. Constitutions instructed that "Every mason shall cultivate brotherly love, and the love of God, and frequent holy church." [11] Additionally, it was required that "at every meeting and assembly they [shall] pray heartily for all Christians." [12]

The charges (i.e., union rules and guidelines) were updated and modified from time to time, but still preserved their Christian tone. For example, 1583 masonic documents declared, "The might of the Father of heaven, and the wisdom of the glorious Son, through the grace and the goodness of the Holy Ghost, yet being three persons and one God, be with us at [our] beginning." [13] The charges of 1686 demanded of masons "that ye shall be true men to God and the holy church." [14] The 1722 charge required that "A mason is obliged, by his tenure, to obey the moral law; and if he rightly understands the art, he will never be a stupid atheist nor an irreligious libertine [a morally unrestrained and ungodly person]" [15] †

Also significant during those years were the mottoes of operative masonry:

> The oldest masonic motto known is "God is our Guide" [1594]; . . . "In the Lord is all our trust" [1688]; . . . the Grand Lodge of England . . . motto was "in the beginning was the Word" . . . [and] "Holiness to the Lord." [16]

By the late 1600s and early 1700s, operative masonry was on the decline; edifices were being built primarily by carpenters rather than stone masons. In an attempt to bolster falling lodge and guild membership, operative masons opened their ranks to those who had never before laid a single stone, admitting them as "honorary" or "non-working" members. As the masonic regulation of 1703 explained: "[T]he

---

† It is because of this 1722 charge that today's Freemasons do not admit atheists into their membership.

privileges of masonry should no longer be restricted to operative masons, but extended to men of various professions." [17]

This era in which masons invited non-masons to join their membership was known as the period of "Accepted Masonry" – accepting into masonic lodges those who had "no artistic or mechanical knowledge" [18] of the trade. As these "accepted masons" were admitted into the lodges of the free masons, the term "Free and Accepted Masonry" was used to describe those lodges. [19] (Today's Freemasons still retain "Free and Accepted" as part of their official name.)

The new "accepted" members included aristocrats and even members of royal families. Soon, other politicians and prominent individuals who desired opportunity to rub shoulders with royalty or

important personages also joined. These new-comers – having no real knowledge of operative masonry – began to speculate and spiritualize on the symbolism of operative masonry and to interpret its symbols and artifacts in an allegorical, moral, and religious manner. As a result, it became known as "speculative masonry."

GIVEN THE OPPORTUNITY, ROYALTY (AND OTHERS) SOON BECAME "ACCEPTED" MEMBERS OF MASONIC LODGES

In 1717 in London, four separate London lodges of "Accepted (i.e., Speculative) Masons" joined together and the following year established their first Grand Lodge, electing and installing a Grand Master over this new form of Masonry. By 1723, these new Masons had developed their own standards to replace the Old Charges that had previously governed operative masons. That first book of standards for Speculative Masonry was written by a Scottish Presbyterian clergyman, the Rev. James Anderson (1679-1739), and was known as "Anderson's *Constitutions*." Amidst all the new teachings, however, speculative masonry preserved and incorporated into their new rituals several traditions from operative masonry (e.g., the three degrees, secret methods of recognition, the requirement of a belief in God, etc.).

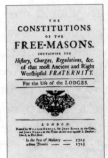

IN 1723, THE REV. JAMES ANDERSON PENNED
THE FIRST WORK OF SPECULATIVE MASONRY

One of the prominent historians of Speculative Masonry describes that form of Masonry:

> Speculative Masonry (which is but another name for Freemasonry in its *modern* acceptation) may be briefly defined as the scientific application and the religious consecration of the rules and principles, the language, the implements, and materials of Operative Masonry to the veneration of God, the purification of the heart, and the inculcation of the dogmas of a religious philosophy. Speculative Masonry, or Freemasonry, is then a system of ethics and must therefore – like all other ethical systems – *have its distinctive doctrines* [many of which, as will be demonstrated later, were quite unChristian]. These may be divided into three classes, namely, the Moral, the Religious [which abandoned its Christian roots and instead embraced the pluralistic and pagan], and the Philosophical." [20] (emphasis and notes added)

As Speculative Masonry was being established, unbelievable claims were incorporated into its newly written works – claims, for example, that Masonry traced its original roots back to Adam, and that God had given Adam certain secrets related to Masonry; that Adam had transmitted these secrets to his sons, and from that generation to the next, down through the history of the Bible and finally on to modern Masons; that those who had been involved in any type of construc-

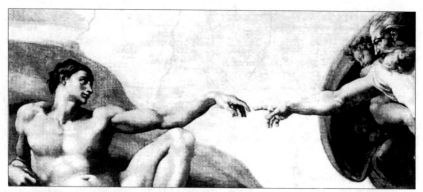

MASONS STATE THAT GOD TRANSMITTED MASONIC KNOWLEDGE DIRECTLY TO ADAM

tion in the Bible (e.g., Noah with the ark, Solomon with the temple, Nehemiah with the wall, etc.) had been Master Masons and knew the "secrets" of Masonry.

ACTIVITIES OF ACTUAL OPERATIVE MASONS IN THE BIBLE INCLUDED
THE BUILDING OF SOLOMON'S TEMPLE (TOP), REBUILDING OF THE WALLS UNDER
NEHEMIAH (BOTTOM LEFT); AND BUILDING THE TOWER OF BABEL (BOTTOM RIGHT)

LONDON Printed; *Anno* 5723.
Re-printed in *Philadelphia* by special Order, for the Use
of the Brethren in *NORTH-AMERICA.*
In the Year of Masonry 5734, *Anno Domini* 1734.

Reproduced in Fac-simile by *the* R. W. Grand Lodge *of* Pennsylvania.
In *the* Year *of* Masonry 5906: *Anno Domini* 1906.

AN EXAMPLE SHOWING BOTH THE MASONIC DATES (5734 & 5906),
AND ALSO THE TRADITIONAL CHRISTIAN DATES (1734 & 1906)

Speculative Masons even began to date their publications by their own calendar system, counting their years from the time of Adam – ostensibly the first Mason and therefore the father of their organization – rather than from the time of Christ. Thus, a Masonic book published in the Christian year 1813 will actually show the year 5813 on its title page (Masons add 4,000 years to the current year to establish the year of their Adamic calendar). This movement of English speculative Lodges of "Free and Accepted Order of Ancient Masons" that began in 1717 grew rapidly, and by 1730, there were 100 speculative lodges in England. [21] From Speculative Masonry sprang up several different paths, or branches, of Freemasonry that eventually became established as today's Freemasonry.

The remainder of this book will examine the three points raised at the beginning of this chapter:

◊   Is American Freemasonry anti-Christian?

◊   What role did Freemasonry play in the lives of the Founding Fathers and the formation of American government?

And based on the answers to the two questions above:

◊   Could America have been established as a Christian nation?

The final conclusion will provide unequivocal evidence that will allow Christians to have great confidence in believing that God _can_ bless America because of her early foundations, and that Christians today do have a sound reason to be involved in the civic and political aspects of the nation with the confident expectation that God _can_ continue to bless America.

CHAPTER 2

Modern Freemasonry and the Founding Fathers

AMERICA WAS SETTLED BY MANY CHRISTIAN GROUPS

For centuries, educators, statesmen, presidents, and judges have – as previously noted – described America as a Christian nation. However, in recent decades, much organized opposition has arisen against that designation. [22] To what evidence do critics point to try to prove their counter-claim? Apart from the writings of modern revisionists, almost none – certainly little to no authoritative evidence. Among Christians critics, perhaps one of the most frequently invoked arguments to "prove" what they allege to be the non-Christian nature of the America founding is to assert that nearly all the Founding Fathers were involved with Freemasonry. According to current works on the subject:

◊ How many signers of the Declaration of Independence were Masons? Fifty-three. [23]

◊ Of the fifty-five members of the Constitutional Convention, all but five were Masons. [24]

◊ Ninety-eight percent of the Founding Fathers of the United States were Masons. [25]

◊ A "Who's Who" of the American Revolution is almost a "Who's Who" of American colonial Freemasonry. [26]

FOUNDING FATHERS WHO SIGNED THE DECLARATION (LEFT) AND CONSTITUTION (RIGHT)

Since American Freemasonry today does express so many anti-Christian teachings, it would be a real concern if the Founding Fathers were indeed Freemasons.

What teachings cause American Freemasonry to be incompatible with Christianity? Consider:

✠ MASONRY: "Jesus of Nazareth was but a man like us, or his history but the unreal revival of an older legend." [27]

  ✝ CHRISTIANITY: Jesus is not just a "man like us," nor is He "the unreal revival of an older legend"; He is Divine; and He is quite real.

✠ MASONRY: "The true Mason. . . . realizes with the divine illumination of his Lodge that as a Mason his religion must be universal; Christ, Buddha or Mohammed, the name means little, for he recognizes only the light and not the bearer. He worships at every shrine, bows before every altar, whether in temple, mosque, or cathedral." [28]

  ✝ CHRISTIANITY: The "light" of Christ and the "light" of Mohammed – or of Buddha – are not the same. In Masonry, universalism is the underlying theological foundation; in Christianity, Christ is the foundation – and contrary to Freemasonry, only one road leads to heaven; in Christianity "there is no other name [Jesus] under Heaven by which men can be saved" (ACTS 4:12) and "I [Jesus] am the way, the truth, and the life; no man comes to the Father but by me [Jesus]" (JOHN 14:6).

✠ MASONRY: "God is as man conceives Him – the reflected image of man himself." [29]

  ✝ CHRISTIANITY: God made man, not vice versa; and man was made in God's image, not God in man's image.

✠ MASONRY: "Scriptures: the literal meaning is for the vulgar only." [30]

  ✝ CHRISTIANITY: The literal meaning of the Scriptures is for all individuals, not just for what Masonry considers the gullible, crude, and inferior.

✠ <u>Masonry</u>: "The good . . . is never separated from the evil. The two must mingle that all may go well." [31] This is the doctrine of dualism, present in the religions of the Medes & Persians as well as in Zoroastrianism and Gnosticism – ancient religions of which Masonry claims to be the modern receiver. [32]

  ✟ <u>Christianity</u>: The doctrine of dualism (that good and evil must always be balanced and equal, and therefore that satan and Jesus are brothers who keep the universe in balance) is rejected; good is <u>not</u> joined to evil, and light is <u>not</u> part of darkness – nor does all go well when they are mixed. In Christianity, light and good prevail over evil and darkness, and good and evil are separate ("What fellowship has righteousness with unrighteousness, and what communion has light with darkness" 2 Corinthians 6:14).

✠ <u>Masonry</u>: "The absolute is reason. . . . If God is, He is by reason." [33]

  ✟ <u>Christianity</u>: God is. Period. His existence makes possible human reason; He is, whether human reason understands Him or not. The statesman Daniel Webster expressed this tenet of Christianity when once he was asked: " 'Mr. Webster, can you comprehend how Jesus Christ could be both God and man?' Mr. Webster, with one of those looks which no man can imitate, fixed his eyes upon him, and promptly and emphatically said: 'No, sir, I cannot comprehend it; and I would be ashamed to acknowledge Him as my Savior if I could

DANIEL WEBSTER

comprehend it. If I could comprehend Him, He could
be no greater than myself; and such is my conviction
of accountability to God – such is my sense of sinful-
ness before Him – and such is my knowledge of my
own incapacity to recover myself – that I feel I need a
superhuman Savior.'" [34]

✠ MASONRY: "Masonry recognizes deity and proceeds only
after asking divine guidance. But it does not specify any
particular deity. You can worship any god you please and
be a Mason." [35]

✝ CHRISTIANITY: (and the Judeo-Christian tradition):
Only one God is worshipped – and that God is <u>not</u>
the universalist deistic god that Masonry denotes as
the "Great Architect of the Universe" (G.A.O.T.U.).

Clearly, much in American Freemasonry today is antithetical to orthodox Christian teachings. Consequently, it would be illogical, and even
oxymoronic, to say that those who embrace beliefs endemically heretical to Christianity could also be orthodox Christians. Therefore, if the
Founding Fathers were members of such a society, then it is appropriate
to question whether they were truly Christians; and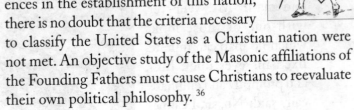
any claim that they founded a nation on Christian
principles would be dubious at best. Christian critics
of Masonry thus logically conclude:

◊ Based upon the evidence of Masonic influences in the establishment of this nation,
there is no doubt that the criteria necessary
to classify the United States as a Christian nation were
not met. An objective study of the Masonic affiliations of
the Founding Fathers must cause Christians to reevaluate
their own political philosophy. [36]

◊ [T]he Revolutionary War and the nation's government
were structured by the tenets of Freemasonry, not God's
Word. It was an unholy alliance at best. [37]

All of this seems reasonable – but only if the Founding Fathers were Freemasons. However, what if they were not?

Yet how can it be otherwise? After all, Thomas Jefferson, Alexander Hamilton, John Adams, James Madison, Charles Carroll, John Jay, Samuel Adams and so many other prominent Founding Fathers were all Masons, weren't they? No! They definitely were not! In fact, not a single one of those individuals was a Freemason – nor were so many of the others often alleged to be members of that organization.

Historical documents unequivocally prove that each of the claims about Masonry and the Founding Fathers that appeared at the beginning of this chapter are patently false. Furthermore, contrary to popular opinion (and what in many cases can only be called both Masonic and Anti-Masonic propaganda), it is historically and irrefutably demonstrable that Freemasonry was <u>not</u> a significant influence in the formation of the United States. This fact is readily confirmed by reputable historians – even reputable Masonic historians – who have taken the time to investigate the actual records, rather than simply to repeat what others have erroneously claimed.

Consider, for example, the work of the Masonic Services Association of North America (hereafter denoted as "MSA"). That organization describes itself as "the servant of Freemasonry" to "provide services to its member Grand Lodges † that they would find difficult to provide for themselves." [38] These scholars research in original Masonic documents and history on behalf of Masonry; and by simply investigating and reporting historical facts, even these Masonic writers have proved conclusively that much of today's pop-culture information about the Founders and Masonry is completely bogus. As they openly acknowledge:

> Sadly, Masons are sometimes counted among the gullible who repeat the tall tale . . . often with a touch of pride. They may be guilty of nothing worse than innocently puffing the

---

† A Grand Lodge is the principal administrative Lodge of a state, above all the regular Lodges in that state.

importance of their fraternity (as well as themselves), but they're guilty nonetheless. The time has come to state the truth plainly and simply! [39]

According to these Masonic scholars: [†]

- JOHN ADAMS and SAMUEL ADAMS: "Masonic tradition has persistently claimed both Samuel Adams and his second cousin, John Adams, as members of the Fraternity... [N]either of the Adamses was a Mason – and this is the conclusion of the authorities of the Grand Lodge of Massachusetts." [40]  MSA further notes that John Adams' own private writings declare that he was "never" a Mason. [41] In fact, John Adams is quoted as saying, "I am not, never was, and never shall be a Free Mason" [42]; and his son, John Quincy Adams, even provided a detailed explanation of the reasons why his father never entered the Masonic organization. [43]

- JAMES MADISON: "[N]o information has as yet been located which  would indicate even possible membership in the Masonic Fraternity." [44] And why have Masonic scholars been unable to locate any such information? Because James Madison himself had resoundingly declared: "I never was a Mason – and no one, perhaps, could be more a stranger to the principles, rites, and fruits of the institution." [45]

- THOMAS JEFFERSON was not a Freemason: "No mention of the Fraternity [Masonry] appears in the millions of words he wrote and which are in print. Strict search has uncovered no evidence." [46]

---

† Since many will probably automatically distrust what a Mason says about the Founders, much non-Masonic historical evidence will also be presented that independently reaches the same conclusions.

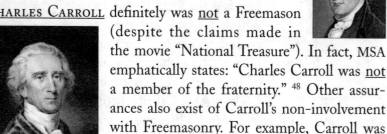

- Concerning <u>ALEXANDER HAMILTON</u>, there is "<u>no</u> evidence of his activity in or connection with the Masonic fraternity." [47]

- <u>CHARLES CARROLL</u> definitely was <u>not</u> a Freemason (despite the claims made in the movie "National Treasure"). In fact, MSA emphatically states: "Charles Carroll was <u>not</u> a member of the fraternity." [48] Other assurances also exist of Carroll's non-involvement with Freemasonry. For example, Carroll was an active and a devout practicing Catholic (the only Catholic signer of the Declaration of Independence); the Catholic Church was (and still is) one of the fiercest opponents of Freemasonry, with over fifteen papal pronouncements having been issued against Freemasonry since 1738. [49] As a practicing Catholic, Carroll closely observed these papal pronouncements; in fact, to have done otherwise could have resulted in his excommunication from the church and, under Catholic doctrine, the eternal damnation of his soul.

- MSA also asserts that <u>JOHN JAY</u> was <u>never</u> a Mason. [50]

There are dozens of similar examples of Founding Fathers who today have wrongly been associated with Freemasonry. [51]

Is this to say that none of the Founding Fathers were Freemasons?

No; some were (they will be identified shortly). However, several of the few who were Masons actually had only minimal contact or involvement with Freemasonry – a fact often ignored by today's Masonic (and Anti-Masonic) propagandists. For example, signer of the Constitution John Dickinson became a Mason on January 11, 1780, but his membership was followed by the notation in the Masonic records: "Never since appeared

JOHN DICKINSON

WILLIAM HOOPER

JAMES MCHENRY

in Lodge." [52] Similarly, signer of the Declaration William Hooper became a Freemason, but then the Lodge of which he was a member ceased to exist, [53] and no records have been found of his attending any other Lodge. And Constitution signer James McHenry became a Freemason on May 21, 1806; but his entry in the records is followed by the notation, "Struck off, 1809," [54] after only three years in the organization.

Yet, notwithstanding the fact that (1) most of the Founders were not Masons; and (2) many who were (such as Dickinson, Hooper, McHenry, and others), were at best inactive; today many nevertheless blindly assert that Masonry was a major influence on the Founders during the formation of American government. That makes as much sense as saying that someone who attended church or prayed or read their Bible only a few times in their lifetime was a strongly dedicated religious individual.

So, if most of the Founders were not Freemasons, then how many were? Of those who signed the Declaration of Independence, a <u>maximum</u> of one in six (16%) could have been Freemasons; [55] and of the delegates to the Constitutional Convention that formed the U.S. Constitution, a <u>maximum</u> of one in four (25%) could have been Freemasons. [56] These numbers represent the maximum number possible and include not only the inactive Masonic Founders but also those with inconclusive evidence of alleged Masonic activity; those with indisputable evidence of having been Freemasons actually represent a much lower percentage than the maximum indicated. (To understand why there is a variance in the percentages, read the text accompanying the two footnotes in this paragraph.)

Beyond the fact that only a few Founding Fathers were Freemasons, today it is rarely considered (or even realized) that American

Freemasonry has undergone radical changes since the eighteenth century, when a few Founders were members. To compare today's Masonic beliefs and practices with those of two centuries ago is to compare night and day. Therefore, before further examining the Founders and Freemasonry, it is important to be aware of the significant changes that have occurred in that organization over the past two centuries.

CHAPTER 3

The Historic Periods in the Progression of American Freemasonry

P erhaps the simplest way to grasp the concept of the historical and theological changes that have occurred in American
Freemasonry since the Founding Era is to recall the changes that
have occurred with other organizations from that era – such as
American Methodism. Founded in the 1740s by John & Charles
Wesley and George Whitefield, early Methodism was characterized
by numerous beliefs and practices that today would be anathema to
many Methodist congregations – including the overtly evangelical
nature of the denomination at that time, its outdoor camp meetings and revivals, and its tendency for demonstrative behavior that
observers in that day described as "emotionalism" and "fanaticism."
It is highly unlikely that the Wesleys or Whitefield (were they still
alive today) would be invited into the modern pulpits of most United
Methodist Churches because of the significant doctrinal disagree-
ments that would now exist.

It is just as unlikely that the Quaker Founding Fathers of two
centuries ago (such as Declaration signer Stephen Hopkins and
Constitution signers John Dickinson, Thomas Mifflin, Jacob Broom,
and George Clymer), or that the Episcopal Founding Fathers (such as
Declaration signers Francis Hopkinson, Elbridge Gerry, and Robert
Morris, and Constitution signers including Rufus King, Gouverneur
Morris, William Samuel Johnson, and others), would affiliate themselves with today's Episcopalians and Quakers who now embrace
pro-homosexual and pro-abortion positions that are anathema to
traditional Christianity (yes – homosexuality and abortion indeed
were topics of consideration in the Founder's generation).

Over the past two centuries, large portions of these denominations (and others) have experienced significant doctrinal shifts
away from their previously held orthodox Christian beliefs, values,

and teachings; to impute the positions of today's groups back to the Founding Era produces a completely inaccurate result. The same is true with American Freemasonry, which has undergone a considerable corruption of belief and practice in its nearly three centuries in America.

Generally speaking, the evolution of the institution of Freemasonry can be divided into distinct epochs (each of which will be briefly introduced below and some of which will be discussed in greater detail in subsequent chapters). Yet even when a different belief or practice was introduced into Masonry so as to mark the beginning of a new epoch, it still was a number of years before that new practice became so widely accepted as to become a representative characterization of general Masonic practices during that period.

◊ **PERIOD I: ORIGINAL AMERICAN MASONRY.** From the 1730s, through the American Revolution, and until approximately 1813, American Freemasonry was an organization that not only adhered to but even _required_ orthodox Christian doctrinal teachings as part of its practices. (A subsequent chapter will present the irrefutable documentation of this truth.)

Incidentally, an error of many critics examining this period – and an error that will also be addressed in detail later – is the tendency to assess American Freemasonry during the Founding Era by pointing to the practices of the highly deistical, paganized, and secularized European Freemasonry of the same time period. That likeness is no more accurate than comparing the American Republic with the French Republic; both were republics, but the similarity ends with the word "republic." As Thomas Jefferson forcefully proclaimed:

> [T]he comparisons of our governments with those of Europe are like a comparison of heaven and hell. [57]

Numerous Founders made clear that Europe and America had little in common; [58] and the same dissimilarity that existed between the European and American governments also existed in regards to Freemasonry – a point that will be abundantly documented later.

◊ **PERIOD II: THE CORRUPTING OF MASONIC BELIEFS.** Following a major philosophical shift in English Freemasonry in 1813, a few lodges in American Freemasonry began to embrace a less Christian and more pluralistic belief system. It was during that time that Freemasonry began aggressively moving forward and overtly describing itself as a system of "speculative masonry," [59] attaching an esoteric "spiritual" meaning to all aspects of operative masonry. Therefore, the tools of operative masons became "spiritually" symbolic. For example, the mason's level was cast as a symbol of universalism, representing "the Fatherhood of God . . . the Brotherhood of Man, and treat[ing] all the brethren of a common spiritual faith"; [60] the common gavel was to be used to "break off . . . all the vices and superfluities of life"; [61] the trowel became a pluralistic symbol to "spread the cement of brotherly love . . . [that] unites us into one sacred band"; [62] etc. American Masonry was moving

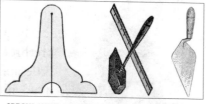

SPECULATIVE MASONRY IMPUTED A SPIRITUAL MEANING TO THE LEVEL, GAVEL, TROWEL, ETC.

away from orthodox Christianity and embracing a form of spiritism, universalism, and mysticism.

◊ **PERIOD III: MASONIC DEMISE.** By 1825, American Freemasonry had changed so dramatically both in its spiritual and philosophical beliefs that an organized national movement emerged against Freemasonry – a movement led by prominent Christians in both Church and State. The movement began as the result of the alleged Masonic murder of Captain William Morgan of Batavia, New York, following his announced intent to publish a work exposing what Masonry had become. That alleged murder involved an intricate coordination, first of Masons who committed the deed and then of Masonic officeholders and judges who refused to punish the Masonic perpetrators. Freemasons were thus shown to be

WILLIAM MORGAN

a fraternal band beyond the constraints of law and even the most basic teachings of Christianity.

A number of America's prominent elder statesmen who had been associated with Masonry in its earlier years denounced the changes that had occurred in that organization and recanted their own affiliation. One was William Wirt (1772-1834), Attorney General of the United States. Wirt had become a Mason early in life but later became an active crusader against Masonry. He commented on the dramatic changes that had occurred in Masonry during his lifetime:

I . . . continually regarded Masonry as nothing more than a social and charitable club, designed for the promotion of good feeling among its members and for the pecuniary relief of their indigent brethren. I have indeed thought very little about it for thirty years. . . . [But now], if this be Masonry – as according to this uncontradicted evidence it seems to be – I have no hesitation in saying that I consider it at war with the fundamental principles of the social compact, as treason against society, and a wicked conspiracy against the laws of God and man, which ought to be put down. [63]

The opposition against what Masonry had become grew rapidly and became officially known as the Anti-Masonic movement; its fervency continued unabated for a full decade (1825-1835). The Anti-Masonic movement even became an organized political party; Anti-Masonic candidates won numerous seats within the legislatures of Northeastern States (including Rhode Island, Connecticut, Massachusetts, and Pennsylvania); governorships (such as in Vermont); and even seats in the U.S. Congress (including the election of John Quincy Adams as an Anti-Masonic member, and more than thirty other Members of Congress [64]). The Anti-Masonic Party also fielded a national presidential candidate in 1832 (William Wirt, Attorney General of the United

States). The movement was substantial, and Anti-Masonic hearings were held across the nation in state legislatures, with numerous laws suppressing Masonry being passed.

During this decade when the fervency of the national Anti-Masonic movement was most intense, there was a mass exodus of Christians from the Lodges. Masonic membership plummeted; many Masonic Lodges closed while others maintained membership numbers only in single digits. For example, in New York, the number of Lodges fell from 480 to 49; [65] in Maine, the number fell from 24 to only 1 – with no members attending. [66] The same fate befell the Lodges in Vermont; and in New Jersey, only 18 Masons attended the statewide meeting in 1839. [67] This trend was repeated in state after state; and although Masonry suffered less in the southern states, the Anti-Masonic movement had a significantly deleterious and near-fatal impact on American Freemasonry.

◊ **PERIOD IV: MASONIC REVIVAL.** By 1835, the national fervor of the Anti-Masonic movement was largely expended. The Masonic

institution barely survived the Anti-Masonic onslaught, but survive it did; it even revived over subsequent decades. For example, in 1835, there were only 49 Lodges remaining in New York; but by 1850, there were 172; and by 1860, the number had risen to 432; [68] the number of Lodges in Massachusetts during this time increased from 56 to 116. [69] The same was true

A MASONIC PARADE

with the other States; American Freemasonry had withstood the assault, and not only recovered but even expanded.

As Freemasonry's growth began anew during the 1840s and 1850s, it began under a different leadership – a leadership that was not only non-Christian but even anti-Christian and pagan. This new leadership established the anti-Christian practices and teachings that today's critics rightfully characterize as being blasphemous to Biblical orthodoxy. Most influential in establishing the new Masonic philosophy during this period were the two men called "The Fathers of Modern American Freemasonry": Albert Mackey (1807-1881) and Albert Pike (1809-1891).

Concurrent with the resurgence of Freemasonry under its new philosophy was a second Anti-Masonic movement. The first movement involved both the pulpit and the Statehouse, but the second movement lacked the sustained political force of the first. One political figure who tried unsuccessfully to regain that original Anti-Masonic fervor was

U.S. Rep. Thaddeus Stevens (1792-1868), an abolitionist and a leading figure during Reconstruction. An Anti-Mason during the first movement, Stevens had been in the Pennsylvania legislature and championed a number of Anti-Masonic bills. However, Stevens was unable to rekindle either the zeal or effectiveness of the first movement. The second Anti-Masonic movement, rather than involving governors and legislators as in

REP. THADDEUS STEVENS

THE REV. CHARLES FINNEY   THE REV. D. L. MOODY

the first movement, primarily involved clergymen such as the Rev. Charles Finney (president of Oberlin College), the Rev. D. L. Moody, the Rev. Jonathan Blanchard (president of Wheaton College), the National Christian Association (led by Methodist ministers N. D. Fanning and C. H. Underwood), as well as other ministers and ministries.

◊ **PERIOD V: MODERN MASONRY.** In the 20TH century, American Freemasonry achieved widespread respectability within the community.

SEVEN 20TH CENTURY U.S. PRESIDENTS HAVE BEEN MASONS, INCLUDING (FROM TOP LEFT TO BOTTOM RIGHT) TEDDY ROOSEVELT, WILLIAM HOWARD TAFT, WARREN HARDING, FRANKLIN DELANO ROOSEVELT, HARRY TRUMAN, LYNDON BAINES JOHNSON, AND GERALD FORD

Aiding this positive Masonic public image was the fact that many visible 20th century leaders were Freemasons, including a number of Presidents (Teddy Roosevelt, William Howard Taft, Warren Harding, Franklin Delano Roosevelt, Harry Truman, Lyndon Baines Johnson, and Gerald Ford), [70] Supreme Court Justices (Stanley Reed, William Douglas, Robert Jackson, Harold Burton, Fred Vinson, Tom Clark, Earl Warren, Potter Stewart, Thurgood Marshall, and nearly a dozen others), [71] Senators (including Robert Byrd, Everett Dirksen, Sam Ervin, John Glenn, Jesse Helms, and Trent Lott), [72] and many U.S. Representatives as well as Governors and state leaders. During this period, the Freemasons made themselves widely known for philanthropic and charitable involvements with crippled children, burn centers, and college football; they were also frequent and visible participants in community parades, and sponsors of a popular circus.

Notwithstanding Masonry's wholesome public image, many denominations still vigorously oppose a Christian's association with it because of its many anti-Christian teachings. In fact, in Roman Catholic Cardinal Bernard Law's 1996 letter to U.S. Bishops explaining why Freemasonry was incompatible with Catholicism, he listed many of the Christian denominations that officially oppose involvement with or membership in Freemasonry. He explained:

> [T]he Catholic Church is hardly the only Christian body to recognize the essential difference between the Masonic and Christian religions. In fact, most Christians around the world belong to churches which forbid or discourage Masonic affiliation. . . . Eastern Orthodox churches characterized Freemasonry as a "false and anti-Christian system." This remains the position of Orthodoxy. Other groups hostile to Lodge membership include many branches of Lutheranism, the Christian Reformed Church, most Pentecostals, the Church of the Nazarene, the Seventh-Day Adventists, the Holiness churches, the Quakers, the United Brethren in Christ, the Mennonites, the Free Methodists, the Church of the Brethren, the Assemblies of God, the Wesleyans, the Regular Baptists, the Salvation Army, and significant minorities in such mainline churches as the Episcopal. [73]

However, the same pastoral letter notes that not all Christian denominations officially oppose Freemasonry:

> For millions of other American Protestants, such as Baptists, Methodists, Presbyterians and Episcopalians, dual membership in the church and the lodge is acceptable. Individual members, however, may have reservations about the compatibility of the Grand Architect of the Universe and the triune God. [74]

American Freemasonry reached its peak membership in the 1950s but has been steadily declining since. [75] (There were almost 4 million Masons in 1959; today, there are well below 2 million. [76]) Freemasonry has not caught on among younger Americans; its current official teachings remain anti-Biblical and heretical.

Of the five periods listed above, two are worthy of closer examination: the first (demonstrating the early Christian nature of Freemasonry) and the fourth (demonstrating the birth and the current anti-Christian teachings of the modern institution).

CHAPTER 4

Early American Freemasonry Part 1: Embracing Orthodox Christianity

A perusal of important writings of early American Freemasonry irrefutably documents its uncompromisingly Christian nature. Consider, for example, the Masonic *Ahiman Rezon* (the title is taken from the Hebrew). First printed in 1756, this work established American Masonic "constitutions," or rules of governance. That early authoritative Masonic guidebook set forth a model prayer for use in American lodges:

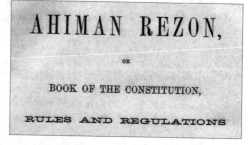

Most holy and glorious Lord God. . . . in Thy name we assemble and meet together, most humbly beseeching Thee to bless us in all our undertakings, that we may know and serve Thee aright, that all our doings may tend to Thy glory and the salvation of our souls. . . . This we most humbly beg, in the name and for the sake of Jesus Christ, our Lord and Savior. Amen. [77]

Would this prayer be presented as a model prayer for American lodges today? Absolutely not. In fact, a current Masonic guidebook, *The Masonic Ritualist,* gives a clear and opposite directive:

In a well-ordered lodge, Jesus is *never* mentioned except in vague, philosophical terms. Prayers are *never* prayed in His name, and when scriptures are quoted in the ritual, *all references to Him are simply omitted*. . . . Albert Mackey (after Albert Pike the highest Masonic authority) calls this changing of the scriptures "a slight but necessary modification." [78] (emphasis added)

This is the position of Freemasonry at large; † it is also the position of Scottish Rite Freemasonry (the branch of Masonry that offers most of the "higher" degrees in Masonry). In fact, this "anti-Jesus-in-prayers" stance is even the position of the current York Rite – the branch of Freemasonry that specifically describes itself as being "Christian." [82] Concerning the York Rite, Chaplain

---

† American Freemasonry begins with what is called Blue Lodge Masonry – the lowest level. The Blue Lodge consists of only three degrees: the Entered Apprentice, Fellowcraft, and Master Mason degrees. An entrant must reach the 3rd degree before he can enjoy the "benefits" of Freemasonry. If a Mason decides to pursue the "advanced" or "higher" degrees (and only one out of three American Masons chooses to do so [79]), there are two primary paths. The first is to enter the York Rite (which offers degrees 4 through 13), and the other is the Scottish Rite, which offers a different set of higher degrees (from 4 to 32). A Masonic authority explains the difference between the York and Scottish Rites: "While the York rite, culminating in the Knights Templar degree, refuses admission to any but Christian Masons, the Scottish rite in the United States repudiates any specifically Christian qualification." [80] Probably the most publicly recognizable aspect of the Scottish Rite are the Shriners, the visible social arm of Scottish Rite Masonry, comprised only of 32nd degree Freemasons. (While every Shriner is a 32nd degree Mason, not every 32nd degree Mason is a Shriner. That is, if a 32nd degree Scottish-Rite Freemason so chooses, he may become a Shriner but is not required to do so.) Interestingly, the Shriners are the purely Islamic expression of Freemasonry [81] and are officially called "The Ancient Arabic Order, Nobles of the Mystic Shrine." (There are currently some 150 Scottish Rite Shrines – or Temples – across America.) A 33rd degree is also available through the Scottish Rite, but it is only an honorary degree and cannot be "earned" or bought, as the lower degrees can. It is sort of a Masonic "Medal of Honor" for Masonic services rendered above and beyond the call of normal Freemasonry and is conferred on Masons by their leadership peers. The awarding of the 33rd degree is usually conferred on only 150 Masons per year in the Northern Jurisdiction of the Scottish Rite and 400 per year in the Southern Jurisdiction. The Blue Lodge, York Rite, and Scottish Rite are the most common paths of American Freemasonry.

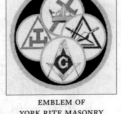

EMBLEM OF
YORK RITE MASONRY

EMBLEM OF
SCOTTISH RITE MASONRY

SHRINER'S FEZ AND ARABIC EMBLEM

Harmon Taylor explains that he "was given only one instruction and was given that one many times"; that directive was that he "was *never, under any circumstance*, to offer prayers in Masonic gatherings in Jesus' name." [83] (emphasis added)

While the current practice of Freemasonry studiously avoids the use of the name "Jesus" and official references to Christianity in Lodge activities or prayers, it was just the opposite for early American Lodges. For example, in 1749, Charles Brockwell reminded a Masonic Lodge that:

> [W]hoever is an upright Mason can neither be an atheist, deist, or libertine; for he is under the **strictest obligation** to be ... a true Christian. [84] (emphasis added)

A 1769 work by moral philosopher Wellins Calcott (1726-1779) – *A Candid Disquisition of the Principles and Practices of the Most Ancient and Honorable Society of Free and Accepted Masons* – similarly declared:

> [A] good Mason is a good man, and a good Christian. [85]

And William Hutchinson's 1775 *Spirit of Freemasonry* similarly stated:

A
CANDID DISQUISITION
OF THE
PRINCIPLES and PRACTICES
OF THE MOST
Ancient and Honourable SOCIETY of
Free and Accepted Mafons;
TOGETHER WITH
Some STRICTURES on the ORIGIN,
NATURE, and DESIGN of that
INSTITUTION.
DEDICATED, BY PERMISSION,
To the moſt Noble and moſt Worſhipful
HENRY DUKE *of* BEAUFORT, *&c. &c.*
GRAND MASTER.
By WELLINS CALCOTT, P. M.

> The Master Mason represents a man under the Christian doctrine, saved from the grave of iniquity and raised to the faith of salvation. As the great testimonial that we are risen from the state of corruption, we bear the emblem of the Holy Trinity as the insignia of our vows. [86]

Even in 1818 (less than a decade before the dramatic turn in Masonic philosophy was manifested), the Christian nature of Freemasonry was still being openly advanced. For example, a Masonic work published that year in New York by Salem Town admonished American Freemasons to be bold in publicizing that "the foundation is laid in *evangelical* truth." [87] That work further declared:

The Scriptures of the Old and New Testament are now received and acknowledged by all Christian nations to be given by Divine Inspiration. Hence, all Christendom quotes the authority of this Book in all matters of religious faith and practice. To this also we appeal as a standard for the correctness and sanctity of our principles. Masonic faith acknowledges the Holy Bible to be the Word of God – that it was written by persons divinely inspired and reveals the whole duty of man. [88]

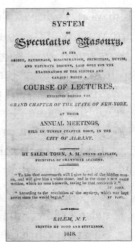

SALEM TOWN'S WORK

(Today, American Masonry would repudiate rather than endorse such positions. In fact, modern Masonry teaches that the Bible is *not* uniquely inspired by God but rather that it is just a book – no different from the Koran (Islam), Vedas (Hinduism), Tipitaka (Buddhism), or the religious book of any other faith. [89])

That 1818 Masonic work then concluded:

[A]bove all, it is not, neither can it be a secret, that a good Mason is of necessity, truly and emphatically, a Christian. [90]

(The endorsing preface to that work was written by Dewitt Clinton – Grand Master of the Lodge of New York. Clinton was a U. S. Senator and introduced the 12th Amendment to the Constitution. Additionally, he was an active Vice-President of the American Bible Society [91] and was outspoken about his Christian faith and about placing the Word of God in the hands of every American. [92])

DEWITT CLINTON

Further confirmation of the Christian nature of early American Freemasonry is seen not only in the official writings of Masonry but also in the numerous sermons preached during Masonic activities – such as those by the Rev. William Smith. (He was a Freemason and an educator who founded Washington College in Maryland [93] and became the Provost of Philadelphia College, the forerunner of the current University of Pennsylvania. [94]) Dr. Smith – a prominent Episcopal theologian – preached a 1778 sermon to the Freemasons of Pennsylvania, reminding them that:

> [W]hen our master, Christ, shall come again to reward his faithful workmen and servants. . . . let us remember that it will be assuredly asked – were we of Christ Jesus? [95]

THE REV. WILLIAM SMITH

Following this sermon, the entire body of Freemasons marched from their assembly hall to Christ Church, where "prayers were read by the Reverend Mr. [William] White; and [an] anthem sung in its

proper place by sundry of the brethren, accompanied with the organ and other instrumental music." [96] (The Rev. William White, 1748-1836, was the outspoken theologian and patriot pastor of Philadelphia's Christ Church, the founder of the Protestant Episcopal Church in America, the first Episcopal Bishop of Pennsylvania, an early promoter of Sunday Schools, and a chaplain to the U. S. House of Representatives. [97])

THE REV. WILLIAM WHITE

Fifteen years later in 1793, the Rev. William Walter, Grand Master for New York, [98] presented a message to the Masonic Lodges in the area and closed with this charge:

> In conclusion, let me remind you, sirs, that ye are Christians. . . . Particularly contemplate the adorable Jesus – that appointed Mediator, the great pattern of human perfection – and tread in His steps. . . . Add, therefore to your faith, knowledge, temperance, patience; to these add godliness; and to godliness, universal charity. For if these things be in you and abound, they will evince

[prove] that ye are not barren nor unfruitful in the knowledge of the Lord, our Savior and our God [2 PETER 1:5-8]. [99]

Five years later in 1798, the Rev. Thaddeus Harris, also a Mason, addressed a Lodge and delivered a sermon on the importance of a Mason "exhibiting and vindicating the principles of Christianity." [100]

Such sermons would not be heard – or even allowed – in American Masonic Lodges today; yet it was a regular practice of American Freemasonry then, and that practice began as early as 1738. [101] (Noted Masonic authority Albert Mackey confirmed that the giving of sermons in Lodges was a practice that was "peculiar to the British and American Freemasons. Neither the French nor German nor, indeed, any continental [European] literature of Freemasonry supplies us with any examples." [102]) Significantly, early American Masonic activities included having Christian clergymen, and no other type, preach Gospel sermons to Masonic members.

THE PREACHING OF GOSPEL SERMONS WAS A REGULAR PRACTICE IN EARLY AMERICAN LODGES

Early American Lodges openly promoted Christian principles and Christian ministries. For example, the Pennsylvania Grand Lodge organized Sunday Schools in its building in order to teach Bible reading to illiterate adults. [103] Because of such activities, one researcher observes:

[A] substantial number of Masonic brothers (and even non-Masons) came to see their order not simply as representing universal principles but a unique order that fulfilled the purposes and proclaimed the truths of Christianity. [104]

Significantly, even Thomas Paine – certainly one of the greatest critics of Christianity – stated in his work, *Origins of Freemasonry,* that:

The Christian religion and Masonry have one and the same common origin. [105]

Paine also claimed that the symbols of the early Masonic Lodges were representative of Christ. [106]

It is unquestionable that early American Freemasonry was Christian in its nature and practices, and included many orthodox Christian ministers in its numbers. In fact, so many devout Episcopalians and Episcopal ministers were members of the organization that gospel ministers of other denominations lamented that American Freemasonry actually served as a missionary arm of the Episcopal Church. For example, a Congregational clergyman, Ezra Stiles (1727-1795; a theologian, scientist, attorney, and president of Yale [107]), openly complained against that Episcopal competition:

THE REV. EZRA STILES

> We see this spirit of Episcopal intrigue already working with great cunning. It has set up and recommended the Fraternity of Free Masons and is pressing them apace into a subserviency and subordination to the great end of increasing the [Episcopal] Church. . . . The Free Masons have already, within about a dozen years, increased from three to 12 or 14 Lodges. [108]

Historians confirm that "[t]he spread of Masonry across the Atlantic formed part of the eighteenth-century Anglicization of American elites" [109] and that "Episcopalian clergymen . . . had been among the first ministers to address and attend American Masonic meetings." [110] It is therefore not surprising that so many of the Masonic Founding Fathers were active Episcopalians – including Constitutional Convention delegates George Washington, John Blair, Rufus King, Edmund Randolph, William Pierce, and Declaration signer William Hooper.

MANY AT THE CONSTITUTIONAL CONVENTION WERE EPISCOPALIAN

Yet, despite the fact that Freemasonry at that time was especially friendly to Episcopalians, ministers from many other denominations were involved; and these ministers also validate the Christian claims made by the early American Masonic Lodges. [111] Given the fact that so many of these leaders were not nominal Christians but were orthodox Christian leaders and noted theologians, it is inconceivable that they would have remained affiliated with Freemasonry had it at that time been hostile to Christ or Christianity, either in belief or practice.

Therefore, after examining Masonic works and Masonic sermons such as those excerpted above (and there are *many* additional examples available), it is clear that orthodox Christianity was an integral part of the Masonic Lodge during the time of the Founding Fathers. Consequently, intellectually honest researchers have concluded that *early* American Freemasonry was *not* antithetical to Christianity.

For example, Dr. Robert Morey (author of a work critical of American Freemasonry – *The Truth About Masons* [112]) examined Masonic literature in chronological order starting with 1723, and concluded that it is "crystal clear that Freemasonry was understood to be a Christian institution until the anti-Masonic movement of 1826." [113] And Tom McKenney (author of multiple works critical of American Freemasonry, including *The Deadly Deception* [114]) similarly concluded:

> [The] fact is, that the institution of Masonry young George Washington joined in 1752 and which survived until fourteen years after his death in 1799, acknowledged and honored Jesus Christ as the Savior of lost mankind and offered prayers in His name. It was not until the formation of the United Grand Lodge of England in 1813 that Jesus was downgraded to the status of merely one of the exemplars [models] and prayers became "universal," making no mention of Him. [115]

Why was Jesus "downgraded" in 1813? Because in that year, the English Grand Lodge (the mother of the American Lodges) decided in favor of the admission of individuals of other faiths; [116] as a consequence, the emphasis on Christianity and a Christian God was removed and replaced with a new emphasis on a general, more universal and all-inclusive God that would be inoffensive to people of other religions and faiths. [†] That change in English Masonic policy – which was eventually embraced by American Masonry [118] (but only well after the death of George Washington and most of the Founders) – brought sharp criticism from American Christian organizations. [119]

Today, probably the one aspect of Masonry with which most individuals are familiar is Masonry's use of blood oaths. Therefore, when it is argued that American Freemasonry began with a Christian viewpoint, how can that claim be reconciled with Masonry's use of blood oaths? (William Morgan had exposed the abominable Masonic blood oaths in his 1825 work describing the rituals of Masonry, and these blood-oaths have since continued as an integral part of Masonic beliefs and practices. [120]) [††]

MORGAN'S 1825
EXPOSÉ OF MASONRY

[†] Even though an entirely Jewish Lodge had been formed in New York City as early as 1769, [117] there was no movement away from the Christian nature of American Freemasonry. That early Jewish Lodge existed unmolested and unthreatened within an otherwise Christian organization. However, the post-1813 decision to alter organizational beliefs to embrace non-Judeo-Christian beliefs represented a major philosophical and theological change.

[††] In those rituals, the Mason first promises to "never reveal any part . . . of the secrets, art, and mysteries of ancient Free Masonry." [121] He then pronounces this oath:

CANDIDATE UNDERGOING INITIATION RITES

> I do most solemnly and sincerely promise and swear, . . . binding myself under no less penalty than to have my left breast torn open and my heart and vitals taken from thence and thrown over my left shoulder and carried into the valley of Jehoshaphat, there to become prey to the wild beasts of the fields and vultures of the air, if ever I should prove willfully guilty of violating any part of this my solemn oath . . . so help me God. [123]

Farther along in the Masonic ritual, the Mason next binds himself with these words:

> I do most solemnly and sincerely promise and swear, . . . binding myself under no less penalty than to have my left breast torn open and my heart and vitals taken from thence and thrown over my left shoulder and carried into the valley of Jehoshaphat, there to become prey to the wild beasts of the fields and vultures of the air, if ever I should prove willfully guilty of violating any part of this my

How can any Christian offer such reprehensible oaths in the name of God – and then invoke God's assistance in upholding those abominable oaths? The only Christian answer is that they can in no way be justified or excused. Just on the evidence of these oaths, how can it possibly be alleged that early American Freemasonry was compatible with Christianity? By the simple fact that these oaths did not exist in Freemasonry at the time of the Founders.

These oaths had been introduced into Freemasonry shortly before they were exposed by William Morgan in 1825 (a revelation that contributed to his death). The previous oath that had been part of Masonry since 1724 (and preceded the blood oaths) was quite different:

> The Freemason's Oath: You must serve God according to the best of your knowledge and institution and be a true liege man [faithful subject] . . . and help and assist any brother as far as your ability will allow. By the contents of the Sacred Writ you will perform this oath. [125]

The perversion that now characterizes the Masonic blood oaths – and which characterized their oaths in 1825 – did not exist at the time of George Washington and the other Founders. In fact, in 1832, U. S. Attorney General William Wirt (a former Mason who became the Anti-Masonic presidential candidate) specifically avowed that he had not taken any such oaths on his entry into Freemasonry, and that those oaths were never taken by George Washington:

> [T]his was not, and could not be Masonry as understood by Washington. The thing is impossible. The suspicion would be parricide [the killing of the country that one cherishes]. [126]

---

solemn oath . . . so help me God. [123]

And in the final of the three blood-oaths, the Mason avows:

I do most solemnly and sincerely promise and swear, . . . binding myself under no less penalty than to have my body severed in two in the midst and divided to the North and South, my bowels burnt to ashes in the center and the ashes scattered before the four winds of heaven, that there might not the least tract or trace of remembrance remain among men or Masons of so vile and perjured a wretch as I should be, were I ever to prove willfully guilty of violating any part of this my solemn oath or obligation . . . so help me God. [124]

American Freemasonry at the time of the Founders rejected the current repulsive oaths. [†] Clearly, the evidence overwhelmingly demonstrates that early American Freemasonry was in no way hostile to the teachings of orthodox Christianity; to the contrary, it jealously embraced those teachings and regularly invited Christian ministers into its Lodges to preach sermons, conduct Christian services, and cooperate in furthering Christian ministry opportunities and services.

---

† In 1986, the Grand Lodges in England finally disavowed and removed these blood oaths from the English rituals; the English York Rite did the same in 1989. [127]

CHAPTER 5

Early American Freemasonry Part 2: The Influence of European Freemasonry and the Illuminati

European Masonry was radically different from that in America (and even that in Great Britain). This fact was made exceedingly clear in 1798 when professor John Robison (1739-1805, a distinguished Scottish scientist and an extensive contributor to the 18th century *Encyclopedia Britannica*) published *Proofs of a Conspiracy Against All the Religions and Governments of Europe*, a work exposing the efforts of the Order of the Illuminati working through European Masonic Lodges. Robison described the group's philosophy:

> PROOFS
> OF A
> CONSPIRACY
> AGAINST ALL THE
> RELIGIONS AND GOVERNMENTS
> OF
> EUROPE,
> CARRIED ON
> IN THE SECRET MEETINGS
> OF
> FREE MASONS, ILLUMINATI,
> AND
> READING SOCIETIES.
> COLLECTED FROM GOOD AUTHORITIES,
> By JOHN ROBISON, A. M.
> PROFESSOR OF NATURAL PHILOSOPHY, AND SECRETARY TO THE
> ROYAL SOCIETY OF EDINBURGH.
> *Nam tua res agitur paries cum proximus ardet.*
> THE FOURTH EDITION.

ROBISON'S WORK INITIATED
A FUROR IN AMERICA

> The Order . . . abjure[s] Christianity and refuse[s] admission into the higher degrees to all who adhered to any of the three confessions [of Christianity]. Sensual pleasures were restored to the rank they held in the Epicurean philosophy. Self-murder [suicide] was justified on Stoical principles. In the Lodges, death was declared an eternal sleep; patriotism and loyalty were called narrow-minded prejudices and incompatible with universal benevolence; continual declamations were made on liberty and equality as the unalienable rights of man. The baneful influence of accumulated property [i.e., private property ownership] was declared an insurmountable obstacle to the happiness of any nation. [128]

Robison accurately charged that the Order of the Illuminati

(founded by German Adam Weishaupt and aided by allies such as the Jacobins [†]) was behind much of the bloody French Revolution and its widespread anarchy. Robison's work dealt heavily and extensively with the work of the Illuminati in Europe, and briefly mentioned in passing that some infiltration of the Illuminati and Jacobins had begun in several other nations, including America. His work was published in London and distributed in England and Europe, but his passing comment about America soon became a focus of attention in the new nation.

ADAM WEISHAUPT

Robison's work was reprinted in New York and Philadelphia; shortly thereafter in Boston, on May 9, 1798, the Rev. Jedediah Morse delivered a sermon to a statewide gathering of Freemasons in which – impelled by Robison's work – he announced that the European Illuminati had infiltrated America and was seeking to overthrow her religious and political institutions. [129] This announcement did not go unnoticed nor was it taken

THE REV. DR. MORSE   lightly, for Dr. Morse was a prominent and well-respected national leader. [††] His alarm spread throughout the country and other prominent clergymen soon preached similar sermons on the apparent imminent danger, including those by the Rev. David Tappan [130] (1752-1803, Professor of Divinity at Harvard) and the Rev. Timothy Dwight [131] (1752-1817,

THE REV. DR. DWIGHT

[†] The Jacobins were political clubs of the French Revolution, formed in 1789; led by Robespierre, they were responsible for the bloody "Reign of Terror" that resulted in the slaughter of tens of thousands of innocents, particularly through the dreaded guillotine.

[††] Dr. Morse (1761-1826) was distinguished in a variety of arenas: as a conservative Christian theologian, he strove to keep Christian doctrine orthodox, uncontaminated by the influence of the Unitarians; as an educator, he introduced the study of American geography into schools and is called "The Father of American Geography"; and as a government commissioner under President James Monroe, he investigated and reported on ways to improve the conditions of Native Americans.

a military chaplain during the Revolution and the president of Yale).

Some Americans, however, apparently found no evidence of the existence of any such group in America and were dubious of the charges. Therefore, on November 29, 1798 (six months after Morse's sermon in which he warned of the Illuminati coming to America), Morse preached a second sermon [132] in which he offered some verification (although only through hearsay) of what he had charged in his first sermon:

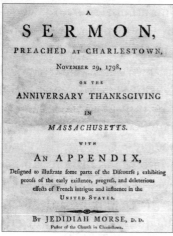

A

SERMON,

PREACHED at CHARLESTOWN,

November 29, 1798,

on the

ANNIVERSARY THANKSGIVING

in

MASSACHUSETTS.

with

An APPENDIX,

Designed to illustrate some parts of the Discourse ; exhibiting proofs of the early existence, progress, and deleterious effects of French intrigue and influence in the UNITED STATES.

By JEDIDIAH MORSE, D.D.

Pastor of the Church in Charlestown.

DR. MORSE'S SECOND SERMON

The probable existence of Illuminism in this country was asserted in my last discourse of May last. The following fact, related by a very respectable divine – while it confirms what is above asserted – shows that my apprehensions were not without foundation: "In the northern part of this state (Massachusetts) as I am well informed there has lately appeared and still exists under a licentious leader, a company of beings who discard the principles of religion and the obligations of morality, trample on the bonds of matrimony, the separate rights of property, and the laws of civil society, spend the Sabbath in labor and diversion as fancy dictates, and the nights in riotous excess and promiscuous concubinage as lust impels. Their number consists of about forty, some of whom are persons of reputable abilities and once of decent characters. That a society of this description . . . should be formed in this land of civilization and Gospel light is an evidence that the devil is at this time gone forth, having great influence as well as great wrath. [133]

Many in the public had readily accepted Morse's charges, but some Americans still found no evidence of any conspiracy. Morse, apparently being pressed on the subject, on April 25, 1799, preached a third (and final [134]) sermon [135] in which he pointed back to "Robison's list" (his original source) as his proof for the charge of an Illuminati group in Virginia. Yet, those who investigated Morse's charge never found any evidence to substantiate his claims. †

Yet even Morse's own series of sermons did not cause him to question American Freemasonry in general or alienate him from it; he was rightly able to distinguish between American and European tendencies. In fact, only six weeks after Dr. Morse preached his first sermon announcing the presence of the Illuminati in America, he delivered a sermon at the Masonic installation of officers in a Lodge. [139] In that sermon, Morse first attacked the Illuminati's "philosophy and influence of exotic origin, in their nature atheistical and licentious, which are secretly undermining and prostrating everything that is excellent in our government, religion, and morals"; he then told the American Masons gathered before him that "I will not suspect any individual in this numerous assembly capable of so much profligacy and baseness." [140] Morse understood that because European Freemasonry had become an enemy to Christianity did not mean that American Freemasonry had.

As a result of the charges originally made by Morse, Americans in general had become conscious of the work of the Illuminati in European Masonic Lodges; many feared a duplication in America. Their concern was logical: Americans were very familiar with American Freemasonry; however, they now knew the perfidy of European Masonry; it therefore became logical to question whether American Freemasonry was like – or was becoming like – the Freemasonry being practiced in Europe; that is, was it susceptible to the same anti-religious influences?

One of those who wondered was the Rev. G. W. Snyder of Fredericksburg, Maryland, an immigrant who wrote directly to George Washington expressing his apprehensions. Rev. Snyder began by explaining to Washington the basis for his anxiety:

---

† Many Americans had initially feared that Dr. Morse might be correct in his claims and quickly moved to halt the efforts of any such group as the Illuminati; however, after two years no one was able to produce any proof validating Morse's claim taken from Robison's original work. [136] By January 1800, leaders such as Thomas Jefferson called Morse's claims "ravings" [137] and had titled him "Illuminati Morse."[138]

I am a German. . . . I came to this country in 1776, and felt
soon after my arrival a close attachment to the liberty. . . . I
am attached – both from the bent of education, and mature
enquiry and search – to the simple doctrines of Christianity,
which I have the honor to teach in public; and I do heartily
despise all the cavils [frivolous objections designed to look
genuine] of infidelity [those who disbelieve the Scriptures and
Christianity]. . . . It was some time since that a book fell into
my hands entitled *Proofs of a Conspiracy* &c. by John Robison,
which gives a full account of a society of Freemasons that
distinguishes itself by the name "of Illuminati," whose plan
is to overturn all government and all religion – even natural;
and who endeavor to eradicate every idea of a Supreme Being,
and distinguish man from beast by his shape only. A thought
suggested itself to me: that some of the lodges in the United
States might have caught the infection. . . . Upon serious re-
flection, I was led to think that it might be within your power
to prevent the horrid plan from corrupting the brethren of
the English lodge over which you preside. [141]

This letter by Rev. Snyder (in which
Snyder enclosed a copy of Robison's
work for Washington's perusal) initiated
a sequence of correspondence between
the two. A month after receiving the
letter, Washington responded to Synder:

I have heard much of the nefarious
and dangerous plan and doctrines
of the Illuminati, but never saw the
book until you were pleased to send
it to me. . . . [T]hanks for your kind
wishes and favorable sentiments – except to correct an error
you have run into, of my presiding over the English Lodges
in this country. The fact is, I preside over none – nor have I

been in one more than once or twice within the last thirty years. I believe notwithstanding, that none of the Lodges in this country are contaminated with the principles ascribed to the Society of the Illuminati. With respect I am, sir, your obedient humble servant, George Washington. [142]

(Notice Washington's strong assertion of his relative non-involvement in Masonry; today, an opposite view is presented – largely by Masonic propagandists who wish to wrap themselves around the patriot-hero Washington in order to make their institution appear as mainstream as possible; radical anti-Masons similarly love to herald Washington as the poster-child of Masonry to "prove" their claim that America was founded by cultic leaders and therefore could not have involved Christian principles. Both sides ignore Washington's own assertions. In fact, erroneous pictures have even been made of Washington presiding over a Virginia Lodge – something he did not do.)

AN EARLY PICTURE SHOWING WASH-
INGTON PRESIDING OVER A VIRGINIA
LODGE – A COMPLETE MYTH

Since a month lapsed before Washington penned his reply to Snyder, several weeks passed without Snyder having received any word from Washington. Still very concerned about the possible danger to America, Snyder therefore wrote a second even more fervent letter to the former President. (Washington's reply to Snyder's first letter crossed in the mail with Snyder's second letter.) In that second letter, Snyder told Washington:

I have since been more confirmed in the ideas I had suggested to you concerning an order of men who in Germany have distinguished themselves by the names of Illuminati – German Union – Reading Societies – and in France by that of the Jacobin Club (that the same are now existing in the United States). It also occurred to me that you might have had ideas to that purport when you disapproved of the meetings of the Democratic societies [†] which appeared to me to be a branch of that order, though many members may be entirely ignorant of the plan. [146]

Two weeks later, having received Washington's reply to his first letter, Snyder wrote the President for the third time, this time repeating his claim of foreign intrigue in America, and specifically pointing to "the anarchical and seditious spirit that showed itself in the United States from the time M. Genet and Fauchet [††] (who

---

[†] Washington believed that the "Democratic Societies" were behind the 1794 Whiskey Rebellion against which he led the American military in order to suppress an insurrection by fellow Americans. Washington talked about these Societies to a number of leaders and individuals. For example, to Henry Lee, he wrote: "I consider this insurrection [the Whiskey Rebellion] as the first formidable fruit of the Democratic Societies. . . . That these societies were instituted by the artful and designing members (many of their body I have no doubt mean well, but know little of the real plan), primarily to sow the seeds of jealousy and distrust among the people, of the government, by destroying all confidence in the administration of it. . . . I see – under a display of popular and fascinating guises – the most diabolical attempts to destroy the best fabric of human government and happiness that has ever been presented for the acceptance of mankind." [143] And in a letter to the U.S. Supreme Court Chief Justice John Jay, Washington noted that "the self-created [Democratic] Societies which have spread themselves over this country have been laboring incessantly to sow the seeds of distrust, jealousy, and of course discontent, thereby hoping to effect some revolution in the government." [144] Then to Burgess Ball, Washington charged that the Democratic Societies attempted "to spread their nefarious doctrines, with a view to poison and discontent the minds of the people against the government . . . and that all the wicked and abominable measures that could be devised (under specious guises) are practiced to sap the Constitution." [145] Washington was open in his condemnation of the doctrines and goals of groups like the Democratic Societies, the Jacobins, and the Illuminati.

[††] Snyder is here referring to two incidents that occurred in 1793 and 1795. In 1793, the French sent ambassador Edmond Charles Genet to America; Genet attempted to stir up hostile feelings between Americans and President Washington. In 1795, while French Diplomat Joseph Fauchet was in America, charges were made public that he was bribing American officials to prevent the passage of Jay's Treaty, a treaty that would reduce tensions between America and Great Britain. The French were at war with Great Britain and wanted to keep the Americans roused against the English. (In 1813 – long after the time of the public charges and Rev. Snyder's letters pointing to these incidents – the American officials were completely exonerated and the alleged bribery incident disproved.) While

EDMOND GENET

the Americans in that incident were later cleared, the French government – permeated with the influence of the Illuminati, the Jacobins, and the Democratic Societies – nevertheless continued in subsequent incidents (including the X, Y, Z affair in 1798, and the naval war of 1798-1800) to attempt to undermine American government.

certainly is of the Order) arrived in this country and propagated their seditious doctrines." [147]

Washington then responded to the Rev. Synder's second and third letters, telling him:

> It was not my intention to doubt that the doctrines of the Illuminati and principles of Jacobinism had not spread in the United States. On the contrary, no one is more fully satisfied of this fact than I am. The idea I meant to convey was that I did not believe that the Lodges of Freemasons in this country had, as societies, endeavored to propagate the diabolical tenets of the first or the pernicious principles of the latter (if they are susceptible of separation). That individuals of them may have done it, and that the founder or instrument employed to found the Democratic Societies in the United States, may have had these objects and actually had a separation of the people from their government in view [such as in the Whiskey Insurrection in 1794], is too evident to be questioned. [148]

Washington was convinced (and subsequent historians agree) that the American Masonic Lodges were not infected with the European Illuminati philosophy, nor were they akin to European Freemasonry. (As a point of interest, European Freemasons today still look deprecatingly upon American Freemasons as lazy and uninformed. For example, attaining higher degrees in Freemasonry in Europe usually involves a year of study for each degree; in America, a Freemason can advance through 29 higher degrees in a single weekend. Unlike European Freemasons, rare is the American Freemason today who has ever read any Masonic work given him on his initiation, or any work explaining the higher degrees through which he can so quickly advance.)

Orthodox Christian ministers agreed with Washington and did not believe that the American Lodges had become infected with the anti-religious tendencies of the European Lodges. In fact, in late 1799, the Rev. Abraham Clarke (1768-1810) delivered an address to the Grand Lodge of Rhode Island in which he attacked the practices of the

European Lodges, condemning the "sons of darkness in some parts of Europe [who] have endeavored to engraft the scion of faction and the thistle of licentiousness upon the venerable tree of Masonry; this they expected to attain by the establishment of what they falsely denominated new or higher orders [degrees]." [149] The Rev. Clarke spoke to the American Masons about "the adorable Redeemer" and predicted that American Masonry would always remain "at eternal enmity with the immoralities, plots, and conspiracies of a Dr. Weishaupt, Baron Knigge, Hertel [leaders in the Illuminati], † and the whole tribe of modern Deists, Atheists, and Philosophists." [151]

While the French and Germans rejected religion in general and Christianity in particular, Americans cherished and embraced it. For example, the French government led a "campaign of de-Christianization" that "led to the closing of all churches" in France; [152] it rejected the Christian calendar and began its own, rejecting the Judeo-Christian seven-day work week and replacing it with a ten-day work week; [153] and it emphasized that pure morality could be attained apart from any religious influence. [154] George Washington, in his "Farewell Address" of September 17, 1796, succinctly attacked the beliefs that characterized the French, reminding Americans :

> Of all the dispositions and habits which lead to political prosperity, religion and morality are indispensable supports. In vain would

---

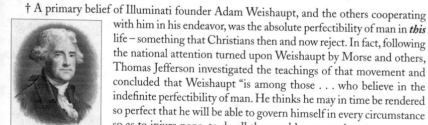

† A primary belief of Illuminati founder Adam Weishaupt, and the others cooperating with him in his endeavor, was the absolute perfectibility of man in *this* life – something that Christians then and now reject. In fact, following the national attention turned upon Weishaupt by Morse and others, Thomas Jefferson investigated the teachings of that movement and concluded that Weishaupt "is among those . . . who believe in the indefinite perfectibility of man. He thinks he may in time be rendered so perfect that he will be able to govern himself in every circumstance so as to injure none, to do all the good he can, to leave government no occasion to exercise their powers over him, and of course to render political government useless" [150] – unfortunately, an ultimate libertarian.

that man claim the tribute of patriotism, who should labor to subvert these great pillars of human happiness. . . . The mere politician . . . ought to respect and to cherish them. A volume could not trace all their connections with private and public felicity. Let it simply be asked, Where is the security for property, for reputation, for life, if the sense of religious obligation desert . . . ? And let us with caution indulge the supposition that morality can be maintained without religion. Whatever may be conceded to the influence of refined education on minds . . . reason and experience both forbid us to expect that national morality can prevail, in exclusion of religious principle. [155]

Obviously, considering the fundamental differences in the philosophy of government and of religion that characterized the two continents, any attempt to impugn early American Freemasonry by linking it to or associating it with European Freemasonry is fatally flawed. The Masonry of the two continents at that time intentionally and aggressively exhibited irreconcilable differences, thereby causing a widespread disdain of European Freemasonry by early American Freemasons (and vice versa).

CHAPTER 6

Early American Freemasonry Part 3: George Washington and Masonry

George Washington – undoubtedly the most recognizable Founding Father associated with Masonry – told the Rev. Snyder that he wanted to . . .

> correct an error you have run into of my presiding over the English lodges in this country. The fact is I preside over none, nor have I been in one more than once or twice within the last thirty years. [156]

Is this statement by Washington accurate? Was he really an inactive nominal Mason?

The validity of Washington's claim is confirmed by an investigation of his Masonic activities. William Adrian Brown, former librarian at the George Washington Masonic Memorial in Alexandria, Virginia, compiled a chronological list of George Washington's life activities in his book *When & Where: A Chronology of the Life of George Washington.* [157] Among Washington's many activities, Brown identifies 29 Masonic activities involving Washington during his 47 years of being a Freemason. Significantly, many of the Masonic activities and contacts in that list were neither initiated by nor participated in by Washington, and several others hardly represent actual Masonic business.

For example, included among the 29 occasions when memorabilia was sent to Washington by other Freemasons, as well as when greetings were extended him by groups of Masons. (Significantly, Washington was given scores of gifts by grateful admirers; some gifts were from Masons. Similarly, Washington was greeted by hundreds of different groups; some were Masonic. Yet, it would be

WHEN & WHERE
A CHRONOLOGY OF THE LIFE OF GEORGE WASHINGTON

unreasonable to select those specific occasions from among hundreds and classify them as genuine Masonic activities.) Also among the events linked to Masonry were public events where Washington was present and at which some Masons were in attendance among the crowd – such as Washington's Inauguration, and public parades. Moreover, included among the Masonic activities linked to Washington were Masonic events at which Washington was not even present – such as on four occasions when various Lodges (often from other states) recommended him as Grand Master (a position he declined in each case), or named him an honorary member of their Lodge.

The genuine Masonic activities in which Washington participated were very few. They include Washington's first becoming a Mason at the age of twenty (November 4, 1752), followed by two more Masonic meetings over the next 10 months (on March 3 and August 4, 1753) in which he completed the three steps of early American Freemasonry. (The higher degrees so common today were rare then. [158] Interestingly, some American Masons condemned higher degrees as being representative of European Freemasonry. [159] Washington took no higher degrees.) The young Washington attended two more Lodge meetings on September 1, 1753, and January 4, 1755. His next Masonic activity recorded by Brownt did not occur until 23 years later in the American Revolution when, on December 28, 1778, he was part of a Masonic parade that marched to Christ Church (Philadelphia) to attend Divine service. During the Revolution, Washington took part in six other Masonic activities or parades (on June 24, 1779, October 6, 1779, December 27, 1779, October 22, 1781, June 24, 1782, and December 27, 1782). Following the Revolution, Washington attended

"PATRIOTS' WINDOW" (STAINED GLASS) AT CHRIST CHURCH, PHILA-
DELPHIA, SHOWING WASHINGTON AND MANY OTHER FOUNDING
FATHERS WHO REGULARLY ATTENDED CHURCH THERE

a Lodge meeting on June 24, 1784; and then on February 12, 1785, he attended the funeral of a fellow Mason. Washington attended no Masonic activities after April, 1789 (except the laying of the cornerstone of the Capitol in September 1793 – an event he attended as President of the United States).

Therefore, in 47 years of being a Freemason, Washington – based on the documentation from Masonic authority William Adrian Brown – participated actively in only 14 genuinely Masonic meetings or activities (many of which were in his early years as a Freemason), therefore confirming his statement to Rev. Snyder that "The fact is, I preside over none [of the Lodges], nor have I been in one more than once or twice within the last thirty years." [160] † Washington simply was not an active Freemason – nor were many other of the Masonic Founding Fathers.

This information is puzzling to many Americans, who have long believed that Washington was an active Mason. The misrepresentation of Washington is aggravated by the numerous paintings depicting him dressed in Masonic regalia – such as those showing him laying the cornerstone of the Capitol. In fact, one can enter the Masonic "House of the Temple" in Washington, D. C., and see a beautiful painting of George Washington – in full Masonic dress – laying the Capitol cornerstone, reinforcing what is already wrongly believed about Washington the Mason. This painting (which appears on the cover of this book) – and so many others like it – is a <u>modern</u> creation, done in 1993 (two

THIS PICTURE OF WASHINGTON-THE-MASON LAYING THE CORNERSTONE IS A MODERN – NOT AN HISTORICAL – CREATION

---

† To be technically accurate, there were actually four documented occasions in which Washington was in a Lodge over those three decades rather than the "once or twice" he mentioned; [161] however his point was about his relative Masonic inactivity, not the exact number of meetings. Four meetings in thirty years is an average of about once a decade – still a very inactive Mason.

centuries after the event) rather than in 1793, when the cornerstone was actually laid. (The modern portrait may be excellent art, but is nothing more than the imaginative historical work of John Melius, an art professor and a 33rd degree Scottish Rite Freemason from Maryland.)

Historians understand that the numerous portraits of "Washington the Mason" or "Washington Laying the Cornerstone" are, by and large, romanticized pieces of propaganda. Consider, for example, what the Architect of the Capitol says about the mural inside the U.S. Capitol entitled "Washington Laying the Cornerstone of the Capitol, 1793," showing Washington in Masonic regalia (a painting done in 1971). According to the description of that mural by the Architect of the Capitol:

THIS U.S. CAPITOL MURAL IS ACKNOWLEDGED
BY THE ARCHITECT OF THE CAPITOL
TO BE AN INACCURATE RENDERING

> Depictions of the first cornerstone ceremony are necessarily the product of the artist's imaginations; no visual record of the event is available as a guide. This mural shows the cornerstone about to be lowered onto a prepared foundation – in *contradiction* of contemporary documents that indicate the stone was placed on the ground. (emphasis added) [162]

Much of what is depicted in such paintings is fallacious; and there are many different Washington-the-Mason portraits . . .

> Those paintings of Washington in his Masonic regalia – which practically all Masons believe were painted from life – are spurious. Ask any honest historian (including honest Masonic historians), and he will tell you that Washington never sat (or "stood") for any such portrait. . . . Those paintings on lodge walls in Masonic Monitors are apocryphal, painted after Washington's death. [163]

ALL OF THE WASHINGTON-THE-MASON RENDERINGS ARE SPURIOUS

Of the numerous Washington-the-Mason portraits, only one was painted during his lifetime; and that one – painted by William Williams – was painted without Washington's blessing. Williams had approached Washington in 1792 to sit for that painting; Washington at that time was a completely inactive Mason and had not been in a Lodge in almost a decade; he flatly refused to sit for the painter. [164] Williams

then offered to paint the portrait for the Alexandria Masonic Lodge (Virginia), the offer was accepted, and Williams (without Washington present) finished it in 1794.

The truth is that Washington's role in Freemasonry is emphasized far beyond what is justified by the facts; modern Freemasonry claims more of Washington than is actually warranted. Washington's Masonic activity was, and still is, grossly exaggerated; he never sat for any Masonic portrait; and his portraits in effusive Masonic regalia are demonstrably

WASHINGTON REFUSED TO SIT
FOR THIS MASONIC PORTRAIT
BY WILLIAM WILLIAMS

spurious. Then why do so many exist? As one art historian explains, those numerous Washington-the-Mason portraits are "used by the order to capitalize on what was only a nominal membership." [165]

Yet, one aspect of Washington's Masonic involvement is worthy of closer examination. Recall from William Adrian Brown's documentation (*When & Where: A Chronology of the Life of George Washington*) that almost half of the Masonic activities in which Washington participated occurred during the American Revolution. Why so many during that period?

Washington's Masonic activities at that time involved what was perhaps the most popular form of Freemasonry during the American Revolution: Military Lodges. These Military Lodges (also called Regimental Lodges) first originated in England in 1732, where they served a major social function. [166] Class standing and caste were closely observed in English social life, thus presenting a significant barrier against camaraderie in British society; in Military Lodges, however, neither rank nor birth caste were officially recognized. The Military Lodges therefore provided the only place where officers (often given their rank on the basis of their social standing rather than their military abilities) as well as regular rank-and-file soldiers could meet together and fellowship as equals. As one authority notes:

> In the British Army . . . [Regimental] Freemasonry forged bonds not just between soldiers but also between soldiers and their officers. Thus, for example, the field lodge of 29th Foot (later Worcestershire Regiment) included two lieutenant-colonels, two lieutenants, and eight privates. The lodge of the 59th Foot, later the East Lancashire Regiment, included a lieutenant-colonel, a major, two lieutenants, a surgeon, a music master, three sergeants, two corporals, and three privates. [167]

Because military personnel from generals to privates could meet together as equals in the Military Lodges, young soldiers could become better known by senior officers and therefore advance more rapidly. [168] These Lodges, introduced into America in the 1750s by the British military during the French & Indian War, provided American soldiers and officers an opportunity to interact with their British counterparts in an informal and less restrictive setting. As one authority explained, "this Freemasonry was to provide an ideal conduit for the kind of rapport and sense of fraternity that tends generally to develop among comrades-in-arms." [169]

Fifty Military Lodges were eventually brought to America by the British [170] – one of which was introduced in 1754 when British troops led by General Edward Braddock arrived in America. [171] A young Colonel George Washington served as Braddock's aide during the campaign against Ft. Duquesne. (Washington's entry into Freemasonry and his appointment as a military

A YOUNG COLONEL GEORGE WASHINGTON (LEFT) SERVED UNDER BRITISH GENERAL EDWARD BRADDOCK (RIGHT) DURING THE FRENCH & INDIAN WAR

officer under the British system had both occurred in 1752. [172]) Significantly, a number of the Masonic American military officers who served

during the Revolution had first become Freemasons while serving in the British military during the French & Indian War. These included American generals Israel Putnam, Hugh Mercer, Joseph Frye, Richard Gridley, John Nixon, David Wooster, and George Washington. [173]

AMERICAN GENERALS SUCH AS DAVID WOOSTER (LEFT) AND ISRAEL PUTNAM (RIGHT) BECAME FREEMASONS DURING THE FRENCH & INDIAN WAR

With so many of America's military commanders having experienced the positive aspects of those British Lodges during the French and Indian War, it is not surprising that shortly after hostilities commenced with Great Britain, the first American Military Lodge was formed – or that it included those who participated in the Revolution's earliest military action. On February 15, 1776, the American Union Lodge was formed for soldiers from Connecticut who had been a key part of the defense of Boston and the Battle of Bunker Hill. [174]

THE FIRST AMERICAN MILITARY LODGE WAS FORMED OF SOLDIERS WHO FOUGHT AT BOSTON AND BUNKER HILL

Eventually, ten Military Lodges were formed within the Continental Army. [175] As one historian noted, "the military lodges . . . were of great value in keeping up the morale of the troops. To afford a place both for the meetings of the military lodges and for religious services, an assembly room or hall was built and dedicated." [176] Wait! These Lodges were used for religious services? Yes – a fact confirmed by the records of American Major-General John Paterson. For example, in describing one such meeting on June 24, 1779, he noted that the "American Union Lodge met" and was "joined by a number of Masonic brethren from the brigades." At the meeting, they "were joined by General Washington and his family. Here addresses were delivered by the Rev. Dr. Hitchcock [1744-1803, a Congregational minister and a chaplain in the Revolution] and Major William Hull." [177]

GEN. JOHN PATERSON

Given the atmosphere and purposes served by these Military Lodges, it is understandable why nearly half of Washington's Masonic activities involved Military Lodges and occurred during the American Revolution.

Based on historical facts, it may be reasonably concluded that: (1) Washington was a Freemason, but an inactive one; (2) Washington had been introduced to Freemasonry during the French & Indian War as a matter of British military tradition, providing one of the few opportunities for equality in a British monarchal society where royalty, class, and caste meant everything; and (3) the meetings in the Military Lodges attended by Washington frequently included religious services, with sermons delivered by Christian clergy.

Chapter 7

Is American Government Permeated with Masonic Symbolism?

[Author's note: In previous chapters, the examination of the issue of Freemasonry and the Founding Fathers has relied solely on historical documentation; this chapter will continue that practice but will also add some of the Author's direct editorial comments following certain quotations. Those comments are denoted by the slightly lighter colored text.]

History unequivocally demonstrates that the Illuminati never took hold in America and that the organization and its beliefs were actively opposed by the American Founders. Yet persistent unfounded charges still abound to the effect that the American Founders were active in the Freemasonic Illuminati and that they inculcated its symbolism throughout American public life.

For example, concerning the physical layout of Washington, D. C., some of the misconceptions that are still given credence include:

◊ [T]he spirit of Freemasonry has been guiding our nation's direction ever since 1776, and . . . this guidance was solidified in 1792 by incorporating Freemasonry symbols into the very street structure of Government Center. . . . [T]he intent of L'Enfante and our Founding Fathers, from the beginning of our country, was to deliberately design Government Center according to Freemasonry principles. [178]

◊ These forefathers embedded Masonic symbols and customs in the . . . layout of buildings in our capital. [179]

◊ [T]he city [Washington, D. C.] was laid out in the form of key Masonic symbols: the square, the compass, the rule, and the pentagram. [180]

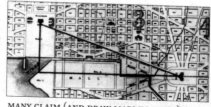

MANY CLAIM (AND DRAW MAPS TO SHOW) THAT WASHINGTON D. C. WAS LAID OUT MASONICALLY

A Masonic pentagram in our nation's capital? Al-
legedly so; and according to Anti-Masonic authorities, the pentagram centers upon the White House:

> Sitting on top of the White House is an
> inverted five-pointed star, or Pentagram. It faces
> North, with the point down in true occult fashion.
> It sits within the intersections of Connecticut and Vermont
> Avenues north to Dupont and Logan Circles, with Rhode
> Island and Massachusetts going to Washington Circle to the
> West and Mt. Vernon Square on the East. The Pentagram,
> or five-pointed star, is, of course, both a Masonic symbol
> and the ancient symbol of witchcraft. With its point facing
> down (or south, when placed on the ground) it is especially
> associated with satanism. [181]

(Author's note: The above thesis is that in 1791 when the Founders
laid out the city, they did so with a pentagram anchored to five specific
locations. The flaw in this thesis is that several of the key locations in
the alleged pentagram mentioned above were neither planned nor built
until almost a century <u>after</u> the Founders (e.g., Mount Vernon Square
was developed from 1845-1945, and Logan Circle from 1874-1877).
Somehow our visionary Founders saw into the future and – at least
according to these writers – knew that someday developments would
arise on the exact location necessary to complete their pentagram!)

Yet, is the Masonic satanic symbolism around which the Founders
laid out the city actually centered upon the White House? Perhaps
it really starts from the Capitol instead:

> Take any good street map of downtown Washington, D.C.,
> and find the Capitol Building. Facing the Capitol from the
> Mall and using the Capitol building as the head or top of
> the Compass, the left leg is represented by Pennsylvania Ave
> and the right leg, Maryland Ave. The Square is found in
> the usual Masonic position with intersections of Canal St.
> and Louisiana Ave. The left leg of the Compass stands on

the White House and the right leg stands on the Jefferson Memorial. The Circle drive and short streets behind the building form the head and ears of what satanists call the Goat of Mendes or Goat's head [the pentagram]! [182]

(Author's note: The Jefferson Memorial – a key to the imagined Masonic symbolism in the city – was not built until 1943, and it never appeared in any of the original 1791 plans of the city. In fact, at that time, the land upon which the Jefferson Memorial now sits was actually underwater in the middle of the Potomac River. The National Park Service – in chronicling the developmental history of the area – accurately notes:

THE ORIGINAL 1791 MAP OF WASHINGTON, D.C.; THE "X" SHOWS THE LOCATION OF THE JEFFERSON MONUMENT

[A]s early as 1830, strict adherence to the [original 1791] L'Enfant plan in the design of the capital city had been abandoned.... The river's edge, which had previously adjoined the mall, was finally [relocated] through the [1875-1901] dredging and reclamation works. [183]

Much of the current layout of the major structures of Washington, D. C. – including the location of the Jefferson and the Lincoln Memorials, which were both in the middle of the Potomac River in 1791 – was actually determined in 1901-1902 by the McMillan Commission. This was a body assembled by Congress and chaired by U. S. Senator James McMillan for the purpose of creating a master plan for the park system of the District of Columbia.

Notwithstanding these facts, according to the critics, our Masonic, satanic Founding Fathers knew that the Jefferson Memorial – underwater and not even thought of by them at that time – would one day sit on land recovered from the river and thus become part of the Masonic symbolism of the city. So, our wise forefathers, with some prescient foreknowledge, therefore laid out the city plans to include underwater as well as land-based sites??? Nonsense! By the way, notice from the attached drawing that the McMillan plan is configured in the shape of a cross (on its side) – although probably not intentionally so planned. Anti-Masons are silent on that obvious "fact" while instead clamoring about an impossible, imaginary pentagram.)

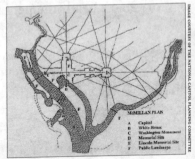

THE 1901 MCMILLAN PLAN – IN THE SHAPE OF A CROSS, NOT A PENTAGRAM

Or perhaps the center of the pentagram [†] is not the White House or the Capitol, but instead something more obscure and sinister:

◊ Freemasons intended that the center of power would be the Temple of Understanding, not the White House! Thus, they located the Temple due North of the obelisk! [184]

[†] Although the pentagram is a simple geometric symbol, it is commonly associated with pagan rites. It was used in ancient nations such as Egypt, Greece, Mesopotamia, and Babylonia, and was related to the worship of the pagan Roman goddess Venus and the pagan Greek goddess Aphrodite. The symbol was also used to represent a talisman (a special charm) in magical rites. And writers have long asserted that when the point of the pentagram is turned upward, it represents good; but when it is turned downward (with two points upward), it is said to represent evil. Thus, its use by satanists in a downward direction, with a symbol of Baphomet (the goat-headed god) inscribed within the pentagram, is why many today consider the pentagram as an evil, sinister symbol. (Anton LaVey, head of the church of satan, adopted the use of this symbol for his church in 1966.)

BAPHOMET, THE GOAT-HEADED GOD (LEFT)
THE GOAT'S HEAD IN A PENTAGRAM (RIGHT)

◊ The center of the pentagram is 16th Street where – thirteen blocks due north of the very center of the White House – the Masonic House of The Temple sits at the top of this occult iceberg. [185]

THE MASONIC "HOUSE OF THE TEMPLE" IN WASHINGTON, D.C.

(Author's note: Apparently the fact that the Masonic "House of the Temple" was not built until 1915 – and the fact that it never appeared on <u>any</u> early plan of the city – doesn't matter to Anti-Masonic conspiracists obsessed with "proving" that Washington is permeated with occultic symbolism. Our Founders nevertheless somehow "planned" that future generations would think of and build this structure on that specific location so that it could become a key part of the satanic pentagram overlaying the city!)

Yet, was it actually a satanic pentagram that the Freemasons incorporated into the city layout? Perhaps it was some other Masonic symbol. What if instead of a Masonic pentagram, the city was actually laid out in the shape of a Masonic cross – or a Masonic octagon?

[T]he Capitol and the White House were each to become focal points of an elaborate geometry governing the layout of the nation's capital city. This geometry, originally devised by an architect named Pierre L'Enfant, was subsequently modified by Washington and Jefferson so as to produce specifically octagonal patterns incorporating the particular cross used as a device by Masonic Templars. [186]

MAP PURPORTING TO SHOW MASONIC SYMBOLS EMBEDDED IN WASHINGTON, D. C.

(Author's note: Evidently these fanatical Anti-Masonic conspiracists forgot that Jefferson was not a Freemason and that Washington had led the American army against American groups promoting the Illuminati and Jacobin philosophy. Yet, apparently these two individuals – so vehemently opposed to the Illuminati – deliberately incorporated its symbolism throughout the city.)

So, is Washington, D. C., laid out according to a Masonic pentagram? Or is it a Masonic cross – or a Masonic octagon instead? Strikingly, those symbols – a five-pointed inverse star, a four-pointed cross, and an eight-sided octagon – are not, geometrically speaking, even remotely close to the same configuration. And is the cross (or the pentagram, or the octagon) centered on the Capitol, the White House, or the Masonic House of the Temple? Disregarding such major problems, Anti-Masonic conspiracists assert that Washington, D. C., <u>must</u> have been laid out on some Masonic symbol – somewhere – in some shape (whatever that shape was)!

TRY LOCATING A "SATANIC PENTAGRAM"

The fact that fixated Anti-Masonic conspiracists can look at the same map and reach radically different conclusions is a significant commentary on the irresponsibility of their claims. If a dozen individuals were given a map of Washington, D. C., and asked to pick the five points that would make an inverse star (i.e., a satanic pentagram), probably no two of them would pick the same five points. This illustrates how arbitrary is the process of "proving" that Washington, D. C., was laid out along some grand Masonic or Illuminati plan.

Yet the Anti-Masonic conspiracists are not content with claiming that the layout of the capital city was Masonic and Illuminati; they further charge that our Founders incorporated satanic Masonic symbolism throughout many other aspects of American government, including the Great Seal of the United States:

◊ [T]he Great Seal of the United States.... appears to be an Illuminati masterpiece. For a good view of the Great Seal, simply take a look at both sides of the U.S. one dollar bill. The pyramid, with 13 levels, was said to represent the 13 colonies, but the association with ancient Egyptian and Babylonian mysticism is apparent.

AN ILLUMINATI SYMBOL?

The eye above the pyramid has been construed to be the All-Seeing Eye of God. However, nothing could be further from the truth. It is the symbol of the Illuminati. [187]

◊ Freemasonry, Rosicrucians, and the Illuminati were the key groups during the late 1700s in America; they produced the occult Unfinished Pyramid as the Obverse Seal of the United States, but kept it secret from 1782 to 1935.... This Government serves the Illuminati!! [188]

◊ [T]he pyramid.... represents the All-Seeing Eye of big-brother government headed up by none other than the god of this world, Lucifer. [189]

◊ On the American dollar bill was printed the "Great Seal" of the United States. It is unmistakably Freemasonic – an all seeing eye in a triangle above a thirteen-stepped, four-sided pyramid, beneath which a scroll proclaims the advent of a "new secular order," one of Freemasonry's long-standing dreams. [190]

What _is_ the meaning of the pyramid and the all-seeing eye in the Great Seal? Are they actually representative of Masonry and the Illuminati? Historical documents provide clear answers to these questions.

The proposal to design a Great Seal for America originated in Congress on July 4, 1776, immediately following the vote to separate from Great Britain and become an independent nation. According to the *Journals of the Continental Congress* for that day:

> *Resolved*, That Dr. [Benjamin] Franklin, Mr. J[ohn] Adams and Mr. [Thomas] Jefferson, be a committee to bring in a device for a seal for the United States of America. [191]

THE COMMITTEE TO PREPARE A SEAL

The composition of this committee is often invoked as the first proof that the Great Seal was indeed Masonic and Illuminati:

◊ Masons designed the Great Seal of the United States with its esoteric symbols. . . . These Masons were Benjamin Franklin, Thomas Jefferson, and John Adams. [192]

◊ On July 4, 1776, Thomas Jefferson (a Mason and Illuminist), John Adams (a Mason), and Ben Franklin (a Mason and Rosicrucian) were appointed by a Committee of the Continental Congress to prepare the Great Seal of the United States. [193]

Yet, since the documentation is unequivocal that neither Jefferson nor Adams was a Mason, then a major part of the supposed foundation on which the Great Seal charge is built actually is non-existent. However, Franklin was a Mason; so did he therefore propose something Masonic for the Great Seal? According to John Adams – one of the three membersof that committee – Franklin proposed:

> Moses lifting up his wand and dividing the Red Sea, and Pharaoh in his chariot overwhelmed with the waters. This motto: "Rebellion to tyrants is obedience to God." [194]

(Also according to Adams, Jefferson proposed: "The children of Israel in the wilderness, led by a cloud by day, and a pillar of fire by night." [195])

Adams' account of Franklin's proposal is substantiated by Franklin's own handwritten proposal (currently in the Manuscript Division of the Library of Congress) that reads:

> Moses standing on the Shore, and extending his Hand over the Sea, thereby causing the same to overwhelm Pharaoh who is sitting in an open Chariot, a Crown on his Head and a Sword in his Hand. Rays from a Pillar of Fire in the Clouds reaching to Moses, to express that he acts by Command of the Deity.

The committee proposed Bible accounts as the basis of the Great Seal; by what stretch of the imagination could they be considered either Masonic or Illuminati? The all-seeing eye _was_ a part of that original proposal, and it was also directly related to the Biblical proposals for the Seal. According to the *Journals of the Continental Congress* for August 20, 1776:

> The committee appointed to prepare a device for a great seal for the United States, brought in the same with an explanation thereof:
>
>> Crest. The Eye of Providence in a radiant triangle, whose glory extends over the shield and beyond the figures.... On the other side of the said Great Seal should be the following device. Pharaoh sitting in an open chariot, a crown on his head and a sword in his hand passing through the divided waters of the Red Sea in pursuit of the Israelites: rays from a pillow of fire in the cloud, expressive of the Divine presence and command, beaming on Moses who stands on the shore, and extending his hand over the sea causes it to overwhelm Pharaoh. Motto. Rebellion to Tyrants is Obedience to God. [196]

PROPOSAL FOR THE FIRST SEAL

The all-seeing eye is specifically described as "the eye of Providence"; it is joined to the account on the other side of the Seal in which God is watching over His people both day and night, and intervening in their behalf to destroy their enemies. The eye in the Great Seal was no pagan, Illuminati, big-brother-government eye; to the contrary, it was the vigilant all-seeing eye of Almighty God, watching over His people.

However, the formation of the Great Seal does not stop with the proposal by Franklin, Adams, and Jefferson; notice that the pyramid is nowhere mentioned in their proposal. This is because that original three-man committee was simply the first committee of several that worked on the design of the Seal over the next six years. [197]

The work of the first committee was tabled by Congress; almost four years later, on March 25, 1780, Congress ordered the report of the first committee to be sent to a new committee of James Lovell, John Scott, and William Houston, with Francis Hopkinson as the artistic consultant [198] (none of those four was a Mason). That second committee issued its recommendations on the Seal, but their proposal also was not approved by Congress. On May 4, 1782, Congress formed a third committee of Arthur Middleton, Elias Boudinot, and John Rutledge [199] (none of whom was a Mason). That committee returned its report, but Congress did not approve that proposal either. Final-

HOPKINSON'S 1780 PROPOSAL

BARTON'S 1782 PROPOSAL

ly, on June 13, 1782, Congress referred all the committee reports to Charles Thomson (Secretary of Congress, 1774-1789) to work as a committee of one and submit a design for the Seal. [200] One week later, on June 20, 1782, after working with artist William Barton (who

WILLIAM BARTON

was not a Mason), Thomson returned his recommendation to Congress, which approved the Seal design the same day. [201]

Charles Thomson is considered the individual most responsible for the completed design of the Great Seal – and this fact provides a second point of "proof" for Anti-Masonic charges that the Seal was indeed Masonic and Illuminati:

CHARLES THOMSON AND HIS 1782 APPROVED SEAL

◊ Charles Thomson, designer of the Great Seal of the United States, was a Freemason. [202]

◊ This design was accepted on May 9, 1782, and referred to Charles Thomson (a Mason). [203]

The only difficulty with these charges is that Charles Thomson was **_not_** a Mason, [204] and therefore, the second major part of the supposed foundation on which the Masonic and Illuminati-symbolism charge rests is also spurious. In fact, not only was Charles Thomson _not_ a Mason, he was actually a noted and orthodox Christian theologian responsible for the *Thomson Bible*. Still sold in Christian bookstores today as one of the most scholarly of all American translations of the Bible, the *Thomson Bible* was America's first translation of the Greek Septuagint into English – a translation project that had occupied seventeen years of Thomson's adult life.

THOMSON'S BIBLE

So why did this theologian include an all-seeing eye and a pyramid as part of the symbolism in the Great Seal? Thomson explained the meaning of those symbols in his final report to Congress:

Charles Thomson's "Remarks and Explanation" Adopted by the Continental Congress, June 20, 1782. . . .

<u>Reverse</u>. A pyramid unfinished. In the zenith, an eye in a triangle, surrounded with a glory proper. Over the eye these words, "Annuit Coeptis." On the base of the pyramid the numerical letters MDCCLXXVI [1776]. And underneath the following motto, "Novus Ordo Seclorum."

Remarks and explanation:

<u>Reverse</u>: The pyramid signifies strength and duration. The eye over it and the motto allude to the many signal interpositions of Providence in favor of the American cause. The date underneath is that of the Declaration of Independence, and the words under it signify the beginning of the new American Era, which commences from that date. [205]

THE GREAT SEAL
(FRONT, TOP; BACK, BOTTOM)
AS APPROVED BY CONGRESS
IN JUNE 1782

Thomson explained – and Congress approved – that the all-seeing eye over the pyramid was the watchful eye of Providence, representing God's "many signal interpositions . . . in favor of the American cause." The Framers truly believed that God had watched over America, and they saw many clear and abundant demonstrations of His intervention.

Benjamin Franklin openly acknowledged this fact at the Constitutional Convention:

In the beginning of the contest with Great Britain, when we were sensible of danger, we had daily prayer in this room for the Divine protection. Our prayers, sir, were heard, and they were graciously answered. All of us who were engaged in the struggle must have observed frequent instances of a superintending

Providence in our favor. To that kind Providence we owe this happy opportunity of consulting in peace on the means of establishing our future national felicity. [206]

Samuel Adams similarly recognized – and recommended:

> The Supreme Ruler of the Universe, having been pleased in the course of His providence to establish the independence of the United States of America, ... we ought to be led by religious feelings of gratitude and to walk before Him in all humility according to His most holy law. [207]

James Madison forcefully announced:

> It is impossible for the pious man not to recognize in it a finger of that Almighty Hand which was so frequently extended to us in the critical stages of the Revolution. [208]

George Washington similarly proclaimed:

> The hand of Providence has been so conspicuous in all this that he must be worse than an infidel that lacks faith, and more than wicked, that has not gratitude enough to acknowledge his obligations. [209]

There is much additional evidence that the Founders believed that God had indeed watched over and preserved America. [†] And just as they believed that God had kept America in His care, they also believed that He watched over every individual for the purpose of reckoning to each his due rewards or punishments at the final day of judgment.

---

† Some may object to the use of "Providence" or "Divine Providence" as being deistic; yet those terms were frequently used by the evangelical Christian pastors of that day. [210] Those pastors described God in similar or identical terms not generally used in today's religious terminology; yet are those pastors to be called "deists" because they used the term "Providence" to refer to God? Hardly. The same is true with the Founders.

The Founders even wrote into many of their State constitutions the requirement that an individual could not hold public office unless he, too, believed that he would account to God for his actions. For example, the 1776 Pennsylvania constitution required:

> And each member of the legislature, before he takes his seat, shall make and subscribe the following declaration, viz: "I do believe in God, the creator and governor of the universe, the rewarder to the good and the punisher of the wicked. [211]

There are many similar examples. [212] It is evident that the Founders believed that God was actively involved: He had watched over America and intervened in her behalf, and He saw the actions of every individual and would call each into direct account for his behavior. Therefore, the historical documentation corroborates the Founders' belief that the all-seeing eye was that of Almighty God and not of some pagan god or Illuminati symbol. Even historians at the Masonic Services Association (MSA) confirm that . . .

> the interpretation of it [the all-seeing eye] by the designers [in 1782] is different from that used by Masons. The eye on the Seal represents an active intervention of God in the affairs of men, while the Masonic symbol stands for a passive awareness by God of the activities of men. [213]

Masonic historians further explain that the all-seeing eye was **_not_** in the earliest works of Freemasonry; and when it later appeared, it was **_not_** within a triangle – as it appears on the Great Seal:

> The first "official" use and definition of the all-seeing eye as a Masonic symbol seems to have come in 1797 with *The Freemasons Monitor* of Thomas Smith Webb – 14 years <u>after</u> Congress adopted the design for the seal. . . . Webb explains the symbol. . . . [and] it is notable that Webb did not describe the eye as being

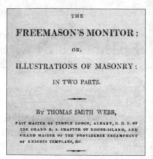

THE

FREEMASON'S MONITOR;

OR,

ILLUSTRATIONS OF MASONRY:

IN TWO PARTS.

By THOMAS SMITH WEBB,

PAST MASTER OF TEMPLE LODGE, ALBANY, G. H. P. OF THE GRAND R. A. CHAPTER OF RHODE-ISLAND, AND GRAND MASTER OF THE PROVIDENCE ENCAMPMENT OF KNIGHTS TEMPLARS, &c.

in a triangle. Jeremy Ladd Cross published *The True Masonic Chart or Hiero-glyphic Monitor* in 1819, es-sentially an illustrated version of *Webb's Moni-tor*. In this first "official" depiction of Webb's symbol, Cross had illustrator Amos Doolittle depict the eye surrounded by a semicircular glory [without any triangle]. [214]

THE 1819 FIRST MASONIC PRINTING OF THE ALL-SEEING EYE

But is there really any difference between the all-seeing eye (a current Masonic symbol) and the all-seeing eye within a triangle (the symbol on the Great Seal)? Yes. According to Masonic scholars:

> When placed in a triangle, the eye went beyond a general representation of God to a strongly Trinitarian statement. [215]

THE 1782 GREAT SEAL HAD THE ALL-SEEING EYE WITHIN A TRIANGLE

This historical evidence – both Masonic and non-Masonic – documents that the all-seeing eye used by Thomson was representative of Almighty God.

But why did Thomson use a pyramid? Recall that the final proposal by Thomson was the synthesis of the work of three previous committees. The pyra-mid had been the product of Francis Hopkinson (a signer of the Declaration of Independence – and not a Mason [216]), who had been assigned to the second committee as its artist.

(By the way, Hopkinson was active in his church, a music director, a choir leader, and the editor of a 1767 hymnal [217] – one of the first purely American hymnals. Hopkinson's work took the one hundred and fifty Psalms and set them all to music so that the Psalms could be sung, much as King David had done over three thousand years before. Many

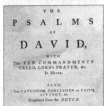

FRANCIS HOPKINSON AND HIS BIBLE HYMNBOOK

consider Hopkinson to be America's first native composer, [218] and he was also a distinguished poet who penned many Christian poems. [219])

Hopkinson had been instrumental in the design of several governmental emblems, including the very first American flag, [220] a number of individual seals used by various governmental departments, [221] and the shield of red and white stripes, thirteen stars, and an olive branch that made its way into the final proposal for the Seal. [222] But what of the pyramid?

During the American Revolution, Hopkinson had been appointed by Congress as Treasurer of the Continental Loan Office (roughly equivalent to today's Secretary of the Treasury), where he both designed and signed continental currency. In his design of the 1778 fifty-dollar colonial note, Hopkinson had used an unfinished pyramid. [223] Thomson included that design in his proposal for the Seal, explaining in his report to Congress that the "pyramid signifies strength and duration." [224]

1778 CURRENCY DESIGNED BY HOPKINSON

Americans in recent generations have not been trained in classical literature – a training that was routine in the Founding Era. Therefore, present-day Americans are not inclined to consider structures from the ancient empires (such as the pyramids), or to be familiar with their heroes (such as Cato, Cicero, and Aeneus), or even with their writers (such as Homer, Virgil, Herodotus, and especially Plutarch – whose massive literary works were studied by every generation of Americans until the 20TH century).

Had we studied ancient history, the reason for the selection of the pyramid would be self-evident: the pyramids were the oldest surviving

structure known to the Founders – perhaps 5,000 years old at that time. Thus, the selection of that symbol communicated the great desire of the Framers: that the American Republic might endure as long as had the great pyramids.

PYRAMIDS: SYMBOLS OF ENDURANCE

Today's Americans might not have chosen a pyramid to place in the Great Seal and probably would not have placed an all-seeing eye over it; yet the choice of those symbols by the Framers does not indicate any type of paganism on their part – and especially not on the part of Thomson. In fact, Masonic historians openly acknowledge:

> Eventually the all-seeing eye came to be used officially by Masons as a symbol for God, but this happened towards the end of the eighteenth century, <u>after</u> Congress had adopted the seal. A pyramid, whether incomplete or finished, however, has <u>never</u> been a Masonic symbol. It has no generally accepted symbolic meaning, except perhaps permanence or mystery. The combining of the eye of Providence overlooking an unfinished pyramid is a uniquely American – not Masonic – icon, and must be interpreted as its designers intended. It has <u>no</u> Masonic context. [225] (emphasis added)

Recall, too, that in Thomson's proposal, the year 1776 was placed at the base of the pyramid – an unfinished pyramid built of thirteen rows of stones, one row representing each of the original thirteen states. Two Latin phrases also appeared with the other symbols. The U. S. Department of the Treasury explains the historical meanings of the various components in the Great Seal:

> The unfinished pyramid means that the United States will always grow, improve and build. In addition, the "All-seeing Eye" located above the pyramid suggests the importance of Divine guidance in favor of the American cause. The inscription *ANNUIT COEPTIS* translates as "He (God) has favored our undertakings," and refers to the many instances of Divine Providence during our government's formation. In addition, the inscription *NOVUS ORDO SECLORUM* translates as "A new order of the ages," and signifies a new American era. [226]

BACK AND FRONT
OF THE GREAT SEAL

Notice: the translation is <u>not</u> "A New World Order" as many Anti-Masons claim [227] (in fact, the literal translation of "A New World Order" would be "Novus Ordo Mundi"); instead, the proper translation of the phrase is "a new order of the ages," speaking of the government of the United States. Recall, too, that Thomson had explained – and Congress approved – that those words "signify the beginning of the new American Era, which commences from that date [1776]." [228] Indeed, America has introduced to the world a new order of government for the ages – a new order of liberty, freedom, and republican self-government.

Anti-Masonic conspiracists often make the mistake of believing that because a particular group uses a symbol, that all others who use that symbol are part of the same group – even if the others had utilized the symbol long before the offending group began to employ that symbol. For example, a common symbol of the New Age religious cult is the rainbow; so does this mean that Noah was a priest of the New Age cult because God originally gave him a rainbow as a sign? Similarly, homosexuals currently use a pink triangle as a symbol of their movement; does it thus follow that all those who drew pink triangles in previous centuries were therefore homosexuals? And were the ancient Pharaohs members of the Illuminati since they built the pyramids? Based on the faulty logic applied by many Anti-Masonic conspiracists, the answer would be "Yes."

As an example of this convoluted thinking, they claim:

> [T]he federalism established in the civil government the Constitution created, is identical to the federalism of the Grand Lodge system of Masonic government created in Anderson's [Freemasonic] Constitutions of 1723. [229]

Notice the illogic: the U. S. Constitution established federalism; the Masonic writings preceding the Constitution also established a type of federalism in the Lodges; therefore, the Constitution must have taken its ideas of federalism from Masonry. Yet federalism had been established in ancient Rome thousands of years <u>before</u> the

Masons, and in ancient Israel thousands of years before Romans. (In fact, early legal authorities actually point to the Jewish federative system – not the Masons – as being illustrative for the American federative government. [230]) Those obsessed with Masonic conspiracies, however, would probably claim that ancient Israel (and even ancient Rome) was actually a part of Freemasonry since it had the same type of federative system as did Freemasons.

When one examines the history of the Great Seal on the basis of historical documentation (as well as common sense), the conspiratorial charges that it is a collage of Masonic symbols produced by Masonic committee members simply cannot be substantiated – not in <u>any</u> measure. In fact, Masonic historians admit:

> Benjamin Franklin was the only Mason on the first design committee, and his suggestions had no Masonic content. None of the final designers of the seal were Masons. [231]

Not content with their discredited claims that the all-seeing eye and pyramid are satanic and Illuminati, Anti-Masonic conspiracists are so obsessed and blinded that they even conclude that the U.S. Capitol is inherently anti-Christian – especially the Congressional Prayer Room. [†] They claim:

> [A] prayer room dedicated to the All-Seeing Eye can be found in the United States Capitol building in Washington, D. C. The movement for its construction was launched in 1952 and the prayer chapel was opened in 1955. The room is located on the House side of the Capitol near the Rotunda. The lighting in this Meditation Room is subdued. The concealed ceiling light focuses on a white oak altar, similar to the U. N. Meditation Room. There are ten chairs facing the altar, just as there are ten chairs in the United Nations Meditation Room. Ten? [Reminiscent] of the beast of Revelation with its ten

---

† To obtain a documentary tour demonstrating the overt Christian influence that permeates the U. S. Capitol, see the work by the author, *A Spiritual Heritage Tour of the United States. Capitol*, available at www.wallbuilders.com.

horns representing ten kings who will give their allegiance to the coming antichrist. Above the altar in the stained glass window the unfinished pyramid with its capstone containing the All-Seeing Eye is prominently displayed. [232]

They therefore conclude that this congressional prayer room is part of a "pseudo-mystical, humanistic, occult system" that "totally excludes Christ as the divine Redeemer" and "reject[s] Jesus Christ, the Son of God" and that the prayer chapel was created in order to "replace Christianity with the cult." [233]

(Author's note: I personally conduct private tours of the U. S. Capitol which are sponsored by congressional Members, and those tours often include the Congressional Prayer Room. Unless you have been in that prayer chapel, you would never know just how egregiously untrue the above claims are.

FIRST, the lighting is not subdued – unless the specific Member wants it so, for the lighting is controlled by a rheostat switch inside the door; the Members of Congress set the lighting where they want it, anywhere from dazzling bright to "subdued." SECOND, the "concealed ceiling light" does not focus on "a white oak altar, similar to the U. N. Meditation Room," but rather on the entire front of the picturesque prayer room – including the kneeling bench, the Bible on the altar, the candelabrum beside the Bible, the stained glass window with its Bible inscription, and the American flag standing

THE CONGRESSIONAL PRAYER ROOM

beside the window. Third, there are not ten chairs facing the altar; there are usually six– and there is barely enough space for those chairs in the tiny room. Fourth, while the symbol from the Great Seal does appear in the stained glass window, it is generally unnoticed; the focus of the window is a rendering of George Washington kneeling in prayer at Valley Forge, with the passage from Psalms 16:1 prominently

displayed around him ("Preserve me, O God, for in Thee do I put my trust"). Displayed above the kneeling, prayerful Washington is the phrase "This Nation Under God," with the names of all fifty states etched into the glass surrounding Washington.

Of all those that I have taken into that prayer room over the years, very rarely is the Great Seal ever noticed, for attention is drawn to so many other prominently visible parts of the prayer room. For example, guests regularly comment on being impressed with the praying Washington, the Scripture surrounding him, and the open Bible on the altar beneath him. In fact, most usually go to the Bible to see the particular passage to which it is opened, but the selected passage changes depending on which Member of Congress was last praying in that room and which passage he or she was reading. By the way, I have been in that room on numerous occasions and have personally prayed in that room with many, many Members of Congress – Members who not only are orthodox Christians but who also are outspoken evangelicals who regularly go to that room to pray to God through His Son, Jesus Christ. There is <u>nothing</u> satanic or universalist or cultic about that congressional prayer room. The Author.)

Characteristic of the many charges often made by Anti-Masonic conspiracists is a general lack of authoritative documentary evidence. They often widely disseminate wild and baseless claims with little or no support other than their own beliefs (and those who believe like them) – reminiscent of an exchange from two contemporary movies.

In "Conspiracy Theory" (Warner Brothers, 1997), a cab driver (actor Mel Gibson) is convinced that everything that occurs is the result of some conspiracy, and a dubious Justice Department prosecutor (actress Julia Roberts) questions him about the conspiracies:

PROSECUTOR: Can you prove any of this?

CABBIE: No! Absolutely not! A good conspiracy is an unprovable one – if you can prove it, then they must have screwed up somewhere along the line.

PROSECUTOR: "They"?

CABBIE: They.

PROSECUTOR: "They" who?

CABBIE: They? Well, "they"; I don't know; that's why they call them "they." They monitor everything – absolutely everything.

PROSECUTOR: Elaborate on "they."

CABBIE: There's lots of groups actually – lots of initials: CIA, FBI, IMF, you name it – "they." But really they're part of the same two opposing factions.

PROSECUTOR: Which are . . . ?

CABBIE: Which are: One – some of them are really wealthy families; their one thing is to maintain stability, or at least that's what they call it. The other group is Eisenhower's industrial military complex. Now they want to maintain instability – or so they say.

PROSECUTOR: So you're saying group one is warring with group two?

CABBIE: Yes; at some levels they're at war; but at other levels, it's the same group. It's really scary!

A similar comedic conspiratorial exchange occurred in the comedy, "So I Married an Axe Murderer" (Columbia Tri-Star, 1993), between a coffee-shop poet (Mike Myers), his father (also played by Mike Myers), and a detective (Anthony LaPaglia):

FATHER: It's a well known fact that there's a secret society of the five wealthiest people in the world known as the Pentaverate who run everything in the world – including the newspapers – and meet tri-annually at a secret country mansion in Colorado known as "The Meadows."

DETECTIVE: So who's in this Pentaverate?

FATHER: The Queen, the Vatican, the Gettys, the Rothchilds, and Colonel Sanders . . . I hate the Colonel with his wee beady eyes and that smug look on his face: "Oh you're going to buy my chicken!"

POET: How can you hate the Colonel?

FATHER: Because he puts an addictive substance in his chicken that makes you crave it fortnightly!

Anti-Masonic conspiracists offer ridiculous claims (such as those listed throughout this chapter) that are easily disprovable with authoritative facts. Ironically, in their furious attempts to "prove" that Masons were behind everything, one observer correctly noted that different Anti-Masonic conspiracists often analyze the same facts but arrive at widely divergent conclusions:

Some Catholic writers claimed that Freemasonry was a Protestant conspiracy, while some Protestants claimed that it was a Catholic conspiracy begun by the Jesuits. But then some Muslim writers say that Freemasonry is an Israeli plot run by Zionist Jews who want to destroy all religions but Ju-

daism. Still others claim that the Fraternity was invented by
the witches of the satanists or luciferians. And lastly, some see
the whole thing as the creation of the Rothchilds and other
Jewish bankers who use the Craft to control the politics and
finance of the world. [234]

Notwithstanding the vocal chorus of conspiratorial claims, historical documentation unequivocally proves that neither the city plan of
Washington, D. C., nor America's government symbols were Masonic. In fact, they were largely the work of non-Masonic Founders;
and even for the few Masonic Founders involved in the planning,
early American Freemasonry considered itself an ally not an enemy
of Christianity. In short, <u>no</u> Founder – whether Masonic or non-
Masonic – made any proposal about America's symbolism that was
in any manner hostile to Christianity.

"Do not call conspiracy everything that these people call conspiracy;
do not fear what they fear, and do not dread it." ISAIAH 8:12

Chapter 8

American Freemasonry the Second Time Around

As noted earlier, American Freemasonry suffered a devastating and near fatal setback during the first Anti-Masonic Movement. However, Masonry survived; by the late 1830s, it was beginning to recover; and throughout the 1840s and 1850s it fully regained its strength.

The two individuals most influential in this recovery and rebuilding were Albert Mackey and Albert Pike. Their writings – filled with beliefs and practices openly heretical to Christianity – not only breathed a new life and spirit into a floundering institution but also revived the Anti-Masonic Movement. (Ironically, the first Anti-Masonic Movement actually helped paganize American Freemasonry: following the mass exodus of Christians from the Lodge during that movement, there was little resistance from those largely non-devout individuals who had remained in the Lodges to the introduction of a new and pagan philosophy by Mackey and Pike.)

Given the influence of these two powerful Masonic giants (and their continuing influence on American Freemasonry today), it is appropriate to become familiar with each.

ALBERT MACKEY

Albert Mackey (1807-1881) was born in South Carolina, where he became a Freemason. He witnessed the anti-Masonic fervor that swept the nation in the 1830s, but unlike so many other Masons, he maintained his membership throughout those difficult years. In 1854, he gave up his chosen profession of medicine to devote his full energy and abilities to re-building American Freemasonry. He rose rapidly through the organization and became

ALBERT MACKEY

Grand Master of the United States – the head of all American Masonic Lodges. Mackey served the last years of his life as Secretary General of the Supreme Council of the 33rd Degree – the highest degree to which a Scottish Rite Mason may rise. The organization Mackey headed is composed only of the equivalent of what might be characterized as Masonic Medal-of-Honor award winners – those who have exhibited extraordinary Masonic achievements, performed exceptional Masonic service, or made remarkable contributions to Freemasonry.

Mackey was perhaps the most prolific Masonic writer ever, penning his first Masonic work in 1845 (*A Lexicon of Freemasonry*) and providing an endless stream of Masonic works until his death in 1881. Some of his notable Masonic writings include *The Mystic Tie* (1849), *Principles of Masonic Law* (1856), *A Textbook of Masonic Jurisprudence* (1859), *Cryptic Masonry* (1867), and *Mackey's Masonic Ritualist* (1869). (The words in the titles of several of his works – "mystic," "cryptic," "ritualist," etc. – indicate the pagan spiritualist aspects Mackey systematically introduced into American Freemasonry.)

ALBERT PIKE

Albert Pike (1809-1891), the second of the Masonic resurrection giants, was born in Boston but moved to Arkansas where he became a journalist and an attorney – one of the richest attorneys in the country. In Arkansas, Pike became active in Freemasonry and rose rapidly, being selected as the Sovereign Grand Commander of the Southern Jurisdiction of Scottish Rite Freemasonry in 1859. Shortly after his selection, the Civil War erupted, and Pike became a Confederate General. After the War, he moved to Washington, D. C., and devoted himself totally into building the Scottish Rite into a forceful and well-organized Masonic entity. (Washington, D. C., is now the home of the Southern Jurisdiction of the Scottish

ALBERT PIKE

Rite – the world's largest Scottish Rite organization – which Pike headed and marshaled into an influential body.)

Pike's *magnum opus* was his infamous *Morals and Dogmas* (1871) in which he standardized the Scottish Rite Masonic degrees from the

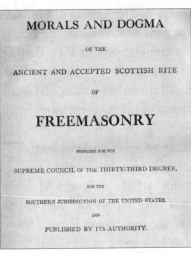

MORALS AND DOGMA

OF THE

ANCIENT AND ACCEPTED SCOTTISH RITE

OF

FREEMASONRY

PREPARED FOR THE

SUPREME COUNCIL OF THE THIRTY-THIRD DEGREE,

FOR THE

SOUTHERN JURISDICTION OF THE UNITED STATES,

AND

PUBLISHED BY ITS AUTHORITY.

PIKE'S 1871 CLASSIC MASONIC WORK

4th to the 32nd, and provided a philo-sophical basis and framework for each. He bestowed titles on several of those higher degrees, includ-ing "Perfect Master" (5th degree), "Prince of Jerusalem" (16th), "Chief of the Tabernacle" (23rd), "Knight of the Sun" (28th), and "Sublime Prince of the Royal Secret" (32nd).

It was in these degree rituals that Pike openly embedded pagan and pluralistic teachings, mixing them with elements of the occult and spiritual mysticism (these are the openly anti-Christian beliefs that have become part of American Free-masonry). [†] Pike claimed that American Freemasonry was the direct receiver of the teachings of the Gnostics, Druids, Essenes, Kaballah, and numerous other long-dead cults [236] – ancient movements against which entire books of the New Testament were written (such as Ephesians to counter teachings of the Essenes, and Colossians to counter teachings of the Gnostics). For sixty years, Pike's work was given to every entrant into Scottish Rite Masonry; even today it is still recommended reading for every American Mason, regardless of the degree attained.

JOHN HENRY COWLES

Pike raised the Scottish Rite from its previous state of obscurity to its current prominent position. Pike is so revered by Masonry that he is one of only two busts displayed at the National Masonic Shrine in Washington, D.C., (the other is of John Henry Cowles, Sovereign Grand Commander from 1921-1952). Today,

---

† Significantly, Pike is also recognized as establishing the rituals of another organization. Following the Civil War, Pike is reported to have been deeply involved with the Ku Klux Klan, serving as one of its officers; he is credited with creating the Klan's rituals. [235]

Pike is described by Masonic historians as "a master-genius of Freemasonry" who "desired that his only monument should be in the hearts
and memories of his Brethren." [237] One eulogist says of Pike that he
"found Masonry in a log cabin and left it in a temple." [238] Because Pike
rewrote the rituals of Masonry and institutionalized them, Masons
claim that "his name will be ever green and of precious memory in all
American Masonry." [239]

Significantly, it is from Pike's work that succinct and virulent anti-
Christian quotes are often drawn by Evangelicals to show why Freemasonry is repugnant to so many Christians today. In fact, an anti-Masonic
book is hardly respectable if it does not cite *Morals and Dogmas* to
prove why the teachings of Freemasonry are incompatible with those
of Christianity (just as this Author did in Chapter 2 of this work).

Yet recall that these loathsome Masonic teachings were <u>not</u> present
in early American Freemasonry; these new and odious Masonic teachings were introduced nearly a century <u>after</u> the American Founding.
In fact, Pike himself openly acknowledged:

> The Freemasonry of the United States is <u>not</u> what it was in
> the days of the Fathers. [240] (emphasis added)

Significantly, modern critics of Freemasonry provide virtually
no offensive quotes from early American Masonic works. Instead,
they (1) regularly cite offensive Masonic works from the period of
Masonic resurgence (or from works of European Freemasonry); and
then (2) wrongly criticize early Freemasons as if they were the Freemasons of the 1870s. This non-scholarly practice has led to numerous
erroneous conclusions regarding the influence of Freemasonry in
the American Founding.

CHAPTER 9
The Founding Fathers, Masonry, and Christianity

While it is appropriate today to question whether a practicing Freemason can also be an orthodox Christian, such a question was not at all pertinent to early American Freemasonry. In fact, if early American Freemasonry had been incompatible with orthodox Christianity, then that lack of Christian orthodoxy would have been evident in the writings of those Founding Fathers who were Masons. Such, however, is not the case; in fact, a cursory examination of prominent Masonic Founders shows the contrary to be true. Some significant examples are presented below.

JOHN HANCOCK

John Hancock (1737-1793) was a Freemason [241] and the son (and the grandson) of a famous Gospel minister. He was the first signer of the Declaration of Independence and twice served as President of Congress. In his own State of Massachusetts, he was made a Senior Major-General and placed at the head of the militia, and was elected the first Governor of Massachusetts – a position to which he was re-elected eight subsequent times. Hancock was instrumental in writing the State's first constitution, with a clause that required an explicitly Christian declaration for public office holders:

I, _____, do declare, that I believe the Christian religion, and have a firm persuasion of its truth. [242]

Is this the work of a Freemason undermining Christianity in the American Founding? Hardly! Furthermore, in his Inaugural Address following his selection as the first Governor of Massachusetts in 1780, he announced:

> Sensible of the importance of Christian piety and virtue to the order and happiness of a state, I cannot but earnestly commend to you every measure for their support and encouragement. [243]

Hancock also urged a "due observation of the Lord's Day" [244] and then issued a statewide call to prayer, asking citizens to pray for "the knowledge of Christianity to spread over all the earth." [245]

This was a frequent request from Hancock; it reappeared in several subsequent prayer proclamations – as in 1782, when he called the State to pray "that the religion of our Divine Redeemer, with all its benign influences, may cover the earth as the waters cover the seas," [246] and in 1783, when he first urged the State to "humble ourselves before Him for our manifold sins" [247] and then asked it to pray that Almighty God "would overrule all events to the advancement of the Redeemer's Kingdom." [248] In his 1790 call for prayer (a decade after he had become Governor), he asked the State first to thank God for "the Holy Scriptures, which are able to enlighten and make us wise to eternal salvation," and then to pray that Almighty God would "cause the benign religion of our Lord and Savior, Jesus Christ, to be known, understood, and practiced among all the inhabitants of the earth." [249] And in 1791, he asked the State to pray that "all may bow to the Scepter of our Lord Jesus Christ, and the whole earth be filled with His glory." [250]

Commonwealth of Massachusetts.

BY HIS EXCELLENCY

John Hancock, Esquire,

GOVERNOR of the COMMONWEALTH of MASSACHUSETTS.

A PROCLAMATION

For a Day of Public FASTING, HUMILIATION and PRAYER.

WHEREAS it hath been the Practice of the People inhabiting the Territory of this Commonwealth, from their first Settlement, at this Season of the Year, unitedly to acknowledge their entire Dependence on the SUPREME BEING, and to humble themselves under a Sense of their utter unworthiness of his Favours, by Reason of their Transgression; and whereas the Practice appears to have a Tendency to cultivate the Fear of God, and a due Regard to its Laws:

I HAVE THEREFORE THOUGHT FIT, by, and with the Advice of the

Would any Governor today – whether a Freemason or not – have the courage of his Christian convictions to be this bold? – or to call his State to prayer for similar Christian purposes? There is no question that John Hancock was a genuine, committed Christian.

RICHARD STOCKTON

Richard Stockton (1730-1781), a signer of the Declaration of Independence, was a Freemason. [251] Like the other signers, he pledged his "life, fortune, and sacred honor" for the cause of American independence; and like the others, he kept his promise. In fact, he was one of nine signers who did not survive the American Revolution.

Captured by the British as a prisoner of war, he was tortured and severely abused. Even though a prisoner exchange eventually secured his release, his health was so crushed that he never recovered; he was dying and he knew it. Understanding this, he placed his temporal affairs in order and penned his last will and testament, giving particular attention to his young children who would never know their father. Notice his strong Christian faith evident in that document:

As my children will have frequent occasion of perusing this instrument and may probably be particularly impressed with the last words of their father, I

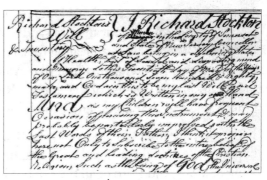

STOCKTON'S HANDWRITTEN WILL

think it proper here not only to subscribe to the entire belief of the great and leading doctrines of the Christian religion – such as the Being of God; the universal defection and depravity of human nature; the divinity of the person and the completeness of the redemption purchased by the blessed Savior; the necessity of the operations of the Divine Spirit; of Divine faith, accompanied with an habitual virtuous life; and the universality of the divine Providence – but also, in the bowels of a father's affection, to exhort and charge them that the fear of God is the beginning of wisdom, that the way of life held up in the Christian system is calculated for the most complete happiness that can be enjoyed in this mortal state, that all occasions of vice and immorality is injurious either imme-diately or consequentially – even in this life. [252]

There is no doubt that this Founding Father – who sacrificed his life for American freedom – was a strong, committed Christian.

JOHN DICKINSON

John Dickinson (1732-1808) helped draft the Declaration of Independence, was a signer of the Constitution, and was a Freema-son. [253] He was a General during the American Revolution and served first as the Governor of Delaware and then of Pennsylvania.

Dickinson had been a member of the 1765 Stamp Act Congress assembled to re-declare American rights and to draw up petitions to the King, appealing for a removal of the tax. When the argument was raised against him that America should submit to Great Britain simply because of the "Divine Right of Kings" doctrine, Dickinson rejected that argument, explaining:

Kings or parliaments could not give the rights essential to happiness... We claim them from a higher source – from the King of kings, and Lord of all the earth. They are not annexed to us by parchments and seals. They are created in us by the decrees of Providence, which establish the laws of our nature. They are born with us; exist with us; and cannot be taken from us by any human power, without taking our lives. [254]

A decade later as America entered the conflict with Great Britain, Dickinson called the nation to seek God:

> Let us therefore, in the first place, humbling ourselves before our gracious Creator, devoutly beseech His divine Protection on us, His afflicted servants, most unreasonably and cruelly oppressed. Let us seriously reflect on our manifold transgressions, and by a sincere repentance and an entire amendment of our lives, strive to recommend ourselves to Divine favor. [255]

Dickinson lived his life as a Christian; and as he faced death, he reaffirmed his personal allegiance to Christ:

> Rendering thanks to my Creator for my existence and station among His works, for my birth in a country enlightened by the Gospel and enjoying freedom, and for all His other kindnesses, to Him I resign myself, humbly confiding in His goodness and in His mercy through Jesus Christ for the events of eternity. [256]

The life, works, and writings of John Dickinson confirm that he was a committed Christian.

ROBERT TREAT PAINE

Robert Treat Paine (1731-1814) was a signer of the Declaration of Independence and a Freemason. [257] He became the first Attorney General of the State of Massachusetts and a Justice on its Supreme Court. He left a clear written record of his faith journey as a Christian. For example, he records his decision to commit his life to Christ:

> I have for some time had a desire to attend upon the Lord's Supper and to come to that Divine institution of a dying Redeemer, and I trust I'm now convinced that it is my duty openly to profess Him least He be ashamed to own me another day. [258]

Significantly, Robert Treat Paine, like his father, became a minister of the Gospel of Jesus Christ; and during the American Revolution, Paine continued his Gospel ministry by becoming a military chaplain to minister to the troops. His military commission charged, "You are therefore carefully and diligently to do and perform the duty of a Chaplain to the said regiment by your public prayers and preaching private exhortations, visiting the sick and in all things as becometh you"; [259] Paine fulfilled that charge.

Robert Treat Paine was both a minister of the Gospel and a patriot; and even at the end of his days, he was still confident about the life in Christ that he would enjoy after his death. He declared:

> I am constrained to express my adoration of the Supreme Being, the Author of my existence, in full belief of His Providential goodness and His forgiving mercy revealed to the world through Jesus Christ, through whom I hope for never ending happiness in a future state. [260]

Founding Father Robert Treat Paine was an outspoken Christian.

JAMES MCHENRY

James McHenry (1753-1816) was a signer of the Constitution and a Freemason. [261] He was also president and founder of the Baltimore Bible Society, [262] which continues today as the Maryland Bible Society. In his work as president of the Bible Society, McHenry drew attention to the critical need to place Bibles in the hands of all people. As he explained:

> [P]ublic utility pleads most forcibly for the general distribution of the Holy Scriptures. The doctrine they preach, the obligations they impose, the punishment they threaten, the rewards they promise, the stamp and image of divinity they bear (which produces a conviction of their truths), can alone secure to society, order and peace; and to our courts

of justice and constitutions of government, purity, stability, and usefulness. In vain, without the Bible, we increase penal laws and draw entrenchments around our institutions. Bibles are strong entrenchments. Where they abound, men cannot pursue wicked courses, and at the same time enjoy quiet conscience. [263]

Clearly, James McHenry was outspoken in his Christian convictions and worked to spread Christian beliefs and the Word of God across America.

GUNNING BEDFORD, JR.

G unning Bedford, Jr. (1747-1812) – a signer of the Constitution – was not only a Freemason but also Grand Master of the Grand Lodge of Delaware. [264] In 1799, he delivered an oration on the death of his close friend and associate, George Washington, in which he openly proclaimed the Christianity of Washington:

To the character of hero and patriot, this good man [George Washington] added that of Christian. All his public communications breathe a pure spirit of piety, a resignation to the will of heaven and a firm reliance upon the providence of God. . . . Although the greatest man upon earth, he disdained not to humble himself before his God, and to trust in the mercies of Christ.[265]

Bedford closed his oration with a spontaneous but powerful orthodox Christian declaration:

Now to the triune God – the Father, the Son, and the Holy Ghost – be ascribed all honor and dominion, forevermore – Amen. [266]

Clearly, Gunning Bedford, Jr. was unashamed of the gospel of Christ and openly embraced and declared orthodox Christian doctrine.

FRANCIS SCOTT KEY

Francis Scott Key (1779-1843), often identified as a Freemason, [267] is known especially
for his authorship of the National Anthem, "The
Star Spangled Banner." It is in the fourth stanza
of the National Anthem that Key articulated the
phrase that served as the basis of our national
motto ("And this be our motto: In God is our
trust"). Key became a Christian early in life and
debated whether to enter the ministry or law; he
eventually chose law, but his love for the ministry
never waned. In fact, he was a regular delegate to
the general conventions of the Episcopal Church,
a manager of the American Sunday School movement, [268] and a vice-president of the American
Bible Society. [269]

KEY'S HANDWRITTEN COPY
OF THE NATIONAL ANTHEM

One of Key's many Christian ministry projects
was the long-term correspondence he carried on
with Congressman John Randolph of Roanoke in
an attempt to bring Randolph to Christ. John Ran-
dolph (1773-1833) was a descendant of John Rolfe and Pocahontas, and

JOHN RANDOLPH

served in Congress under Presidents John Adams,
Thomas Jefferson, James Madison, James Monroe,
John Quincy Adams, and Andrew Jackson. Interestingly, John Randolph was an adherent to the Muslim faith. [270] Over a course of years, Key faithfully
and patiently wrote numerous letters to Randolph,
witnessing to him about Christ and Christianity.
Key's patience with Randolph was eventually re-
warded, for Randolph finally told Key:

I have thrown myself upon the mercy of my Redeemer, conscious of my own utter inability to conceive one good thought
or do one good act without His gracious aid. [271]

John Randolph was overjoyed with his new-found faith. As he told Francis (Frank):

> Congratulate me, dear Frank – wish me joy you need not; give it you cannot – I am at last reconciled to my God and have assurance of His pardon through faith in Christ. . . . [and] for the first time, I understand your feelings and character – and that of every real Christian. [272]

Key, too, was elated, and urged Randolph:

> [M]ay I always hear that you are following the guidance of that blessed Spirit that will lead you into all truth, leaning on that Almighty arm that has been extended to deliver you, trusting only in the only Savior, and going on in your way to Him rejoicing. [273]

Francis Scott Key indisputably was a strong evangelical Christian.

BENJAMIN FRANKLIN

While it is certainly not alleged by this Author that Benjamin Franklin (1706-1790) was a Christian, it is nevertheless demonstrable that this Masonic Founding Father was not anti-Christian. To the contrary, in several recorded instances he was far more pro-religious and pro-Christian than many church-goers today. Franklin was a strident defender of religion in general and of Christianity in particular – pointedly demonstrated by an exchange with anti-religionist Thomas Paine.

Thomas Paine and Ben Franklin became friends well before the American Revolution, and it was with Franklin's help that Paine had emigrated from England to America in 1772. Franklin helped establish Paine in the printing business, where he quickly won the respect of many of the Founders by authoring the political pamphlet *Common Sense*, setting the tone for the American Revolution. Paine authored a number of subsequent works, and fifteen years after *Common Sense*, he decided to reveal his religious views in his *Age of Reason* – an attack on Christianity and religion. (Unfortunately, many of Paine's arguments in that work are still urged today – especially his belief that if religion was to play a role in a nation, that it must be minimized, isolated, and kept separate from public life, including from education, government, law, etc.)

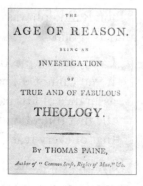

Before publishing the *Age of Reason*, Paine sent a summary of his thoughts on the subject to Franklin, seeking Franklin's candid opinion. After reading Paine's work, Franklin responded with a sharp rebuke:

> I have read your manuscript with some attention. By the argument it contains against a particular Providence (though you allow a general Providence), you strike at the foundations of all religion. For without the belief of a Providence that takes cognizance of, guards, and guides, and may favor particular persons, there is no motive to worship a Deity, to fear His displeasure, or to pray for His protection. I will not enter into any discussion of your principles, though you seem to desire it. At present I shall only give you my opinion, that . . . the consequence of printing this piece will be a great deal of odium drawn upon yourself, mischief to you, and no benefit to others. He that spits against the wind, spits in his own face. But, were you to succeed, do you imagine any good would be done by it? . . . But think how great a portion of mankind . . . have need of the motives of religion to restrain them from vice, to support their virtue, and retain them in the practice of it till it becomes habitual, which is the great point for its security. . . . I would advise you, therefore, not to attempt unchaining the tiger, but to burn this piece before it is seen by any other person. . . . If men are so wicked with religion, what would they be if without it? [274]

One of the nation's most forceful defenses of religion against Paine's attacks was made by Benjamin Franklin! (Ironically, today's critics of religion love to herald Paine's anti-religious words as being typical of the Founders' position on religion; few mention Franklin's pro-religious position, which is much more representative.) What else did Franklin do that might prove that he was not an enemy to religion?

Not only did Franklin suggest a Biblical symbol and a religious motto for America's Great Seal, [275] but he also personally drafted a statewide prayer proclamation for his own State of Pennsylvania, [276] and worked to raise church attendance in the State. [277] Additionally,

he proposed to evangelist George Whitefield that the two start a colony in Ohio (a territory at that time occupied by the French rather than the English) in order to "facilitate the introduction of pure religion among the heathen" and to show the Indians "a better sample of Christians than they commonly see in our [French] Indian traders." Franklin enthused, "In such an enterprise I could spend the remainder of life with pleasure, and I firmly believe God would bless us with success." [278] Franklin also aggressively promoted Christianity throughout public education.

For example, he was instrumental in the early development of education for black Americans, [279] helping

FRANKLIN URGED THE REV. GEORGE WHITEFIELD (TOP) TO JOIN WITH HIM TO START A CHRISTIAN COLONY IN OHIO (EARLY TRADERS' MAP OF OHIO ABOVE)

found a series of schools that trained black students both in academics and in the principles of Christianity. [280] Two decades before founding those schools, Franklin had helped found the University of Pennsyl-

vania for the explicitly declared purpose of
instructing youth in the knowledge of the
Christian religion. [281] He then authored the
famous piece entitled *Proposals Relating to the
Education of Youth in Pennsylvania* in which
he discussed the academic curriculum of that
university, noting that in its history classes:

> History will . . . afford frequent opportunities of showing the
> necessity of a public religion from its usefulness to the public
> [and] the advantage of a religious character among private
> persons . . . and the excellency of the Christian religion above
> all others, ancient or modern. [282]

And it was also Franklin who – at the Constitutional Convention – offered a compelling, Bible-based call for daily prayer and
the establishment of chaplains:

> Mr. President:
>
> The small progress we have made after four or five weeks
> close attendance and continual reasonings with each other
> – our different sentiments on almost every question – . . .
> is methinks a melancholy proof of the imperfection of the
> human understanding. We indeed seem to feel our own
> want of political wisdom, since we have been running about
> in search of it. We have gone back to ancient history for
> models of government and examined the different forms
> of those republics which . . . now no longer exist. And we
> have viewed modern states all round Europe but find none
> of their constitutions suitable to our circumstances. In this
> situation of this Assembly – groping, as it were, in the dark
> to find political truth, and scarce able to distinguish it when
> presented to us – how has it happened, Sir, that we have not
> hitherto once thought of humbly applying to the Father of
> Lights [JAMES 1:17] to illuminate our understandings?
>
> In the beginning of the contest with Great Britain, when
> we were sensible of danger, we had daily prayer in this room

for the Divine protection. Our prayers, Sir, were heard, and they were graciously answered. All of us who were engaged in the struggle must have observed frequent instances of a superintending Providence in our favor. To that kind Providence we owe this happy opportunity of consulting in peace on the means of establishing our future national felicity. And have we now forgotten that powerful Friend?

I have lived, Sir, a long time, and the longer I live, the more convincing proofs I see of this truth: that God governs in the affairs of men. And if a sparrow cannot fall to the ground without his notice [MATTHEW 10:29], is it probable that an empire can rise without His aid? We have been assured, Sir, in the sacred writings, that "except the Lord build the House they labor in vain that build it" [PSALMS 127:1]. I firmly believe this; and I also believe that without His concurring aid we shall succeed in this political building no better than the builders of Babel [GENESIS 11:3-9]. . . .

I therefore beg leave to move that henceforth, prayers imploring the assistance of Heaven, and its blessings on our deliberations, be held in this Assembly every morning before we proceed to business. [283]

And in preparation for his death, Franklin – a famous printer – penned an inscription for his own grave:

The Body of Benjamin Franklin,
Printer,
(like the cover of an old book,
its contents torn out,
and stript of its lettering and gilding,)
Lies here, food for worms.
Yet the work itself shall not be lost,
for it will – as he believed – appear once more,
in a new and more elegant edition,
corrected and amended
by
THE AUTHOR [284]

While Franklin was certainly pro-religious
and pro-Christian, it is unlikely that he was
personally a Christian. Only months before his
death, one of his most ardent admirers – the
Rev. Ezra Stiles, president of Yale – had asked
his old friend:

THE REV. DR. EZRA STILES

> You know, Sir, that I am a Christian, and
> would to Heaven all others were such as I
> am (except my imperfections and deficien-
> cies of moral character). As much as I know of Dr. Franklin, I
> have not an idea of his religious sentiments. I wish to know the
> opinion of my venerable friend concerning Jesus of Nazareth.
> He will not impute this to impertinence or improper curiosity
> in one who, for so many years, has continued to love, estimate,
> and reverence his abilities and literary character with an ar-
> dor and affection bordering on adoration. If I have said too
> much, let the request be blotted out and be no more; and yet
> I shall never cease to wish you that happy immortality, which
> I believe Jesus alone has purchased. [285]

Franklin responded with a surprising reply:

> You desire to know something of my religion. It is the first
> time I have been questioned upon it. [286]

It is regrettable that the first time Franklin had been asked about
a personal belief in and relationship with Jesus Christ occurred just
weeks before his death at the age of 84. Franklin continued:

> I cannot take your curiosity amiss, and shall endeavor in a
> few words to gratify it.   Here is my creed. I believe in one
> God, the Creator of the universe. That He governs it by
> His Providence. That He ought to be worshipped. That the
> most acceptable service we render to Him is doing good
> to His other children. That the soul of man is immortal,

and will be treated with justice in another life respecting its conduct in this. These I take to be the fundamental points in all sound religion, and I regard them as you do in whatever sect I meet with them.

As to Jesus of Nazareth – my opinion of whom you particularly desire, I think his system of morals and his religion, as he left them to us, the best the world ever saw or is like to see; but I apprehend it has received various corrupting changes and I have, with most of the present Dissenters in England, some doubts as to his divinity; though it is a question I do not dogmatize upon, having never studied it – and think it needless to busy myself with it now, when I expect soon an opportunity of knowing the truth with less trouble. . . .

I shall only add, respecting myself, that having experienced the goodness of that Being in conducting me prosperously through a long life, I have no doubt of its continuance in the next, though without the smallest conceit of meriting such goodness. . . . All sects [denominations] here (and we have a great variety) have experienced my good will in assisting them with subscriptions for the building their new places of worship; and as I have never opposed any of their doctrines, I hope to go out of the world in peace with them all. [287]

These are the last words written by Franklin on the subject of religion, and they indicate that he was not a Christian (and had never even previously been questioned about his faith). Nevertheless, that same writing confirms that he considered himself a friend to and ally of Christians. As shown by the documented actions throughout the long life of this Masonic and perhaps _least_ religious Founder, Franklin certainly promoted Christianity much more strongly than do many professing Christians today. Therefore, the claims of today's Anti-Masons that Franklin worked to overthrow religion in America are palpably false.

GEORGE WASHINGTON

A dditional historical proof exists that many of the other Masonic Founding Fathers not mentioned in this section were genuine Christians who adhered to orthodox Christian beliefs; [288] yet the most identifiable of all Masonic Founding Fathers whose faith has not yet been explored is George Washington. And just as his Masonic involvement is today overstated, his abundantly documented Christian faith is understated – or totally ignored. An excellent example of this is seen in the original publication (followed by the recent republication) of the historical work *The Maxims of Washington*.

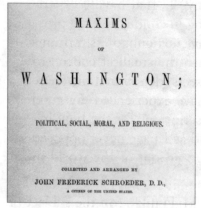

In 1855, John Frederick Schroeder studied all of Washington's available writings and divided Washington's pithy statements into a variety of topical categories. (Washington was a prolific writer; today there are nearly one hundred volumes of his published writings – and this does not include the countless volumes written about him by his friends and contemporaries.) Schroeder compiled Washington's sayings into the book *The Maxims of Washington*, dividing his maxims into four categories: political, social, moral, and religious. [289]

In that book, Schroeder introduced each category of maxims with testimonials about Washington from his contemporaries. These testimonials came from noted individuals who personally knew Washington, including Alexander Hamilton, General Marquis de Lafayette, John Paul Jones, John Hancock, and numerous others.

In the section on Washington's religious maxims, those are numerous individuals who testified about Washington's Christian faith:

◊ U. S. Supreme Court Chief-Justice John Marshall served on Washington's staff during the Revolution; he declared, "He was a sincere believer in the Christian faith and a truly devout man." [290]

◊ Elias Boudinot was a President of Congress during the Revolution (and under President Washington was a Member of Congress, helping frame the Bill of Rights); he declared of Washington: "The General was a Christian." [291]

◊ The Rev. Devereux Jarratt was a Virginia minister who pastored the church where Washington attended and served as a vestryman; he declared that Washington "was a professor of Christianity." [292]

There are similar additional testimonials about Washington scattered throughout the chapter, but there is no doubt that those who knew George Washington personally and unequivocally declared that he was a Christian. In fact, testimonies abounded from Washington's contemporaries confirming his Christianity:

George Washington. . . . respects God's Word, believes in the atonement through Christ, and bears himself in humility and gentleness. [293] THE REV. HENRY MELCHIOR MUHLENBERG, PASTOR; FOUNDER OF THE LUTHERAN CHURCH IN AMERICA

He was a firm believer in the Christian religion . . . . For my own part, I trust I shall never lose the impression made on my own mind in beholding – in this house of prayer – the venerable hero, the victorious leader of our hosts, bending in humble adoration to the God of armies and great Captain of our salvation! [294] JONATHAN MITCHELL SEWELL, SONGWRITER; ATTORNEY

[I]f we cannot aspire at his talents as a General, a President, or a Statesman, we may imitate his virtues as a man, a citizen, and a Christian. [295] ABIEL HOLMES, REVOLUTIONARY SURGEON; HISTORIAN

Christianity is the highest ornament of human nature. Washington practiced upon this belief. . . . He was neither ostentatious nor ashamed of his Christian profession. [296] JEREMIAH SMITH, REVOLUTIONARY SOLDIER; U. S. CONGRESSMAN; GOVERNOR OF NEW HAMPSHIRE

Perhaps the most concise testimony of George Washington's faith comes from Nelly Custis, Washington's adopted daughter. Nelly lived with the Washingtons at Mount Vernon for twenty years, from her childhood until her own marriage. In a letter she wrote to Jared Sparks, a chaplain of Congress, Nelly forcefully declared:

> I should have thought it the greatest heresy to doubt his firm belief in Christianity. His life, his writings, prove that he was a Christian. . . . As well may we question his patriotism, his heroic, disinterested devotion to his country. [297]

Even though his adopted daughter declared that one might as well question the patriotism of George Washington as question his Christianity, nevertheless, through the work of today's secular revisionists, George Washington has wrongly been labeled "deist."

As an example of this revisionism, the original *Maxims of Washington* was recently reprinted in its entirety [298] – that is, almost in its entirety. The difference was that the introduction to each section was changed; and in the section on Washington's religious maxims, the personal, eye-witness testimonies from those who declared George

Washington to be a Christian were replaced by the commentary of a present-day professor claiming that George Washington was a deist, not a Christian. [299]

Revisionist W. E. Woodward similarly asserts:

> The name of Jesus Christ is not mentioned even once in the vast collection of Washington's published letters. [300]

And yet, on June 12, 1779, to the Delaware Indian Chiefs, Washington declared:

> You do well to wish to learn our arts and ways of life, and above all, the religion of Jesus Christ. These will make you a greater and happier people than you are. [301]

Furthermore, in one single document – a well-worn, handwritten prayer book found among Washington's personal writings after his death – the name "Jesus Christ" was directly invoked twelve times; [302] it also appeared numerous additional times throughout that document in other varied forms such as "Jesus," "Lord Jesus," etc.

Additionally, Washington was boldly forthright in promoting Christianity in numerous official writings and orders. For example, on July 9, 1776, he issued an order to the troops that:

> The General hopes and trusts that every officer and man will endeavor so to live and act as becomes a Christian soldier. [303]

And on May 2, 1778, he reminded his soldiers at Valley Forge:

> To the distinguished character of a Patriot, it should be our highest glory to add the more distinguished character of a Christian. [304]

There are numerous other examples to demonstrate Washington's Christian beliefs, including the many documented reports of his extensive prayer activities and of his faithful church attendance, as well as his involvement in positions of leadership in several different Christian churches.

Just as Washington's involvement in Freemasonry is overemphasized, his Christian involvement is underemphasized; he was an active Christian and an inactive Mason.

An honest examination of the writings of the few Founding Fathers who were Freemasons finds no evidence of hostility toward Christianity. To the contrary, the writings of the Founders demonstrate the general unequivocal Christian commitment of those individuals, expressed both in private and in public. †

---

† While the overall body of Founders demonstrates a Christian commitment, there were among them a few select individuals (some Masons and some non-Masons) who expressed anti-religious beliefs, including Ethan Allen, Henry Dearborn, and Charles Lee. However, on the basis of historical documents, of the 200+ individuals considered to be Founders (e.g., signers of the Declaration, drafters of the Constitution, framers of the Bill of Rights, and leading Revolutionary Generals and Governors), perhaps only a dozen (or about five percent) can be characterized as anti-Christian or anti-religious.

CHAPTER 10

Conclusion

Despite abundant historical proof to the contrary, many current writers on the subject of Freemasonry in the Founding Era still wrongly espouse that: (1) virtually every one of the Founding Fathers was a Freemason; (2) early American Freemasonry was no different from modern Freemasonry; (3) American Freemasonry was a hotbed for the Illuminati; and (4) the Founders established America on cultic principles. Based on these erroneous premises, they wrongly conclude:

◊ "[O]ur occult Forefathers" designed America with "latent paganism" and "America was dedicated to . . . satan" to become "the most occult and most powerful nation since Atlantis, nearly 12,000 years ago . . . to lead the world into the Kingdom of the anti-Christ, a kingdom they called the New World Order." [305]

◊ Satanic organizations . . . counted most of the Founding Fathers of America among its membership. [306]

◊ "Paganism, Wicca, WitchCraft and Earth-Centered spirituality are . . . in near perfect harmony with the deist beliefs of many of the Founding Fathers," who worshipped "the Horned God of the Witches." [307]

◊ [O]ur nation was founded, and has operated on and by, the Masonic Order. [308]

◊ [O]ur Founding Fathers, who were Freemasons. . . . intended that Freemasons would determine the political and spiritual direction of the infant United States of America. This direction was to be toward their New World Order. We are now very, very close to this goal today. Thus, our seeds of destruction were sown by our Founding Fathers. [309]

Numerous other similarly ludicrous charges have been made – charges that receive wide publicity and which, regrettably, are today believed by many. Yet, to accept such fables, one must ignore the unequivocal historical facts documented in this book: (1) the overwhelming majority of the Founders were not Freemasons; (2) many who were Masons were at best inactive; (3) the Freemasonry of the Founders is not Freemasonry of today; and (4) the overwhelming majority of both Masonic and non-Masonic Founders were generally orthodox Christians who were very pro-God and pro-Christ in both words and actions.

Anti-Masonic conspiracists who persist in claiming that America was founded as a Masonic or occultic nation, and who make uninformed assertions about the Masonic involvement of the Founders, apparently have been educated beyond their own intelligence. Could they for a moment relax the pre-conceived notions to which they irrationally adhere, they would do well to examine the abundant and irrefutable historical evidence (both Masonic and non-Masonic) of the truth.

There is simply no evidence of any effort to undermine Christianity by the collective group of Founders, or by any part of them; however, there is more than ample evidence to the contrary. After all, it is these same Founding Fathers who started Bible Societies, the American Tract Society, the American Sunday School movement, and many of the evangelical Christian organizations that still exist today. [†]

The historical facts are clear that early American Freemasonry exerted no measurable influence on the American Founding; and even if it had, at that time it was not incompatible with orthodox Christianity. Therefore, the fact that a few of the Founding Fathers may have been involved in early Freemasonry cannot legitimately be used to undermine the otherwise Christian nature of the American Founding. ■

---

† To see a list of the many Christian organizations started by our Founding Fathers, refer to chapter 6 in *Original Intent* by the author, available at www.wallbuilders.com.

Endnotes

1. See, for example, Jim Shaw [33rd Degree, past "Worshipful Master" past "Master of all Scottish Rite Bodies"] & Tom C. McKenney, *The Deadly Deception* (Louisiana: Huntington House, 1988); Jack Harris [former "Worshipful Master"], *Freemasonry: The Invisible Cult In Our Midst* (Towson, MD: Jack Harris, 1983); Claude McClung [Royal Arch Mason, 7th Degree], *Why I left Masonry* (no pub info given); *et. al.*

2. See, for example, "Our Masonic Founding Fathers," *Midnight Call*, October 2005, p. 35; Alexander Holmb, "The Masonic Founding of The United States of America," *Global Insights* (at: http://www.nohoax.com/masonic_founding.htm); Tim Bryce, "An Introduction to Freemasonry" (at: http://www.os2ss.com/connect/masons/present.htm) (accessed on August 10, 2010).

3. EDUCATORS include Noah Webster, "The Schoolmaster to America;" Jedediah Morse, "The Father of American Geography;" and William McGuffey of the famous *McGuffey Readers*; STATESMEN include Elias Boudinot, a President of Congress during the Revolution, and signers of the Declaration Charles Carroll, John Hancock, Benjamin Rush, Stephen Hopkins, Samuel Adams, Alexander Hamilton, Rufus King, John Dickinson, and Roger Sherman; other leaders include General William Eaton, leader of America's first conflict following the American Revolution, and Daniel Webster, the great "Defender of the Constitution"; PRESIDENTS include John Adams, George Washington, John Quincy Adams, Abraham Lincoln, Woodrow Wilson, Zachary Taylor, Harry Truman, Andrew Jackson, William McKinley, Herbert Hoover, Teddy Roosevelt; and JUDGES include Samuel Chase, a signer of the Declaration and a U. S. Supreme Court Justice; original Supreme Court Chief Justice John Jay; Justice Joseph Story; Justice James Kent; Zephaniah Swift, author of America's first legal text. For more information see pages 18-19 of our booklet *The Role of Pastors & Christians in Civil Government* (available from www.wallbuilders.com).

4. B. F. Morris, *The Christian Life and Character of the Civil Institutions of the United States* (Philadelphia: George W. Childs, 1864); Daniel Dorchester, *Christianity in the United States* (New York: Hunt and Eaton, 1890); Charles Galloway, *Christianity and the American Commonwealth: or The Influence of Christianity in Making This Nation* (Nashville: Publishing House Methodist Episcopal Church, South, 1898); David Brewer, *The United States: A Christian Nation* (Philadelphia: John C. Winston Company, 1905); Peter Marshall and David Manuel, *The Light and the Glory* (Grand Rapids: Fleming H. Revell Company, 1977); John Eidsmoe, *Christianity and the Constitution: The Faith of our Founding Fathers* (Grand Rapids: Baker Books, 1987); Gary Amos, *Defending the Declaration: How the Bible and Christianity Influenced the Writing of the Declaration of Independence* (Brentwood, TN: Wolgemuth & Hyatt, Publishers, Inc., 1989); David Barton, *Original Intent: The Courts, the Constitution, & Religion* (Aledo, TX: WallBuilder Press, 1996); Stephen McDowell, *America, a Christian Nation? Examining the Evidence of the Christian Foundations of America* (Charlottesville: Providence Foundation, 2005); etc.

5. In the December 8, 1730, edition of the *Pennsylvania Gazette*, it was noted that "several Lodges of Freemasons" had been "Erected in this Province." See also "Pennsylvania Masonic History," *Grand Lodge of Pennsylvania* (at: http://www.pagrandlodge.org/programs/masedu/qa/41-50.html) (accessed on August 10, 2010). Although Masons were meeting together in Pennsylvania, Boston organized the first American Lodge officially recognized by the

Grand Lodge of London on July 30, 1733 (see Melvin Maynard Johnson, *Freemasonry In America Prior To 1750* (Cambridge: Caustic-Claflin Company, 1917), p. 22).

6. "History of Freemasonry," *MasterMason.com* (at: http://mastermason.com/rfire/masonry/history.html#Modern)(accessed on August 10, 2010); See also S. Brent Morris, "Scottish Rite Membership: A Silver Lining In The Clouds," *The Scottish Rite Journal of Freemasonry, Southern Jurisdiction, USA*, AUGUST, 2002 (at: http://www.srmason-sj.org/web/journal-files/Issues/aug02/morris.htm); and "Masonic Education," *Fisher Family Home Page* (at: http://users.1st.net/fischer/SHORT15.HTM) (accessed on August 10, 2010).

7. "Freemasonry and the Catholic Encyclopedia," California Freemason On-Line, 2002 (at: http://www.freemason.org/cfo/may_june_2002/cath2.htm).

8. "Freemasonry," *Wikipedia Encyclopedia* (at: http://en.wikipedia.org/wiki/Freemasonry) (accessed on August 10, 2010).

9. Tom C. McKenney, *Please Tell Me…Questions People Ask About Freemasonry – and the Answers* (Lafayette, LA: Huntington House, 1994), pp. 15-16; See also "History of Freemasonry," *MasterMason.com* (at: http://mastermason.com/rfire/masonry/history.html#Modern) (accessed on August 10, 2010).

10. Joseph Fort Newton, *The Builders* (United States: Supreme Council, 33° Ancient Accepted Scottish Rite of Freemasonry Northern Masonic Jurisdiction, 1973), pp. 108-109.

11. Albert G. Mackey, *A Textbook of Masonic Jurisprudence Illustrating the Written and Unwritten Laws of Freemasonry* (New York: Robt. Macoy, 1859), p. 90.

12. *The Encyclopedia Britannica* (1910), s.v. "Freemasonry."

13. *The Encyclopedia Britannica* (1910), s.v. "Freemasonry," citing from the documents of Grand Lodge MS. No. 1, A.D. 1583.

14. Mackey, *Textbook of Masonic Jurisprudence (1859)*, p. 50.

15. Mackey, *Textbook of Masonic Jurisprudence (1859)*, p. 55.

16. *The Encyclopedia Britannica* (1910), s.v. "Freemasonry."

17. Mackey, *Textbook of Masonic Jurisprudence (1859)*, p. 53.

18. George F. Fort, *The Early History and Antiquities of Freemasonry, As Connected with Ancient Norse Guilds, and the Oriental and Medieval Building Fraternities* (Philadelphia: Robert H. Ball, 1877), p. 137.

19. *The Encyclopedia Britannica* (1910), s.v. "Freemasonry."

20. Albert G. Mackey, *Encyclopedia of Freemasonry* (New York: Masonic History Company, 1924), Vol. II, p. 704.

21. "The History of Grand Lodge," *The United Grand Lodge of England* (at: http://www.grandlodge-england.org/ugle/the-history-of-grand-lodge.htm) (accessed on August 10, 2010).

22. For example see: "ADL Letter to Texas Republican Party," *Anti-Defamation League* (at :http://www.adl.org/religious_freedom/Letter_texas_rp.asp) (accessed on August 10, 2010) and "Faith & Freedom: The Case for Separation of Church and State," *Anti-Defamation League* (at: http://www.adl.org/issue_religious_freedom/faith-freedom/faith_freedom_schools.asp) (accessed on August 10, 2010); and "Is America A 'Christian Nation'?" *Americans United for Separation of Church and State* (at: http://www.au.org/site/PageServer?pagename=resources_brochure_christiannation) (accessed on August 10, 2010).

23. *The New Standard Alphabetical Indexed Bible* [Masonic Edition] (Chicago: Hertel Co., 1951), p. 23. See also Madison C. Peters, *The Masons As Makers of America* (Yonkers: Trowel Publications, 1917), p. 16; "The Esoteric Side of the Founding of America: Understanding the Spiritual Roots of the Founders of the United States," Camp Internet Homeschool

Campus, (at: http://www.rain.org/homeschool/american-history-esoteric-roots-vision-4. html) (accessed on August 10, 2010); Manly P. Hall, *America's Assignment With Destiny* (Los Angeles: Philosophical Research Society, Inc., 1951), pp. 96-97; and Freemasonry and Secret Societies, "What is Freemasonry? What is a Secret Society?" (at: http://www.plim. org/Freemasonp1.htm) (accessed on August 10, 2010).

24. Hall, *Assignment With Destiny*, p. 97; See also Peters, *Masons As Makers*, p. 47; and "What is Freemasonry? What is a Secret Society?" *Freemasonry and Secret Societies* (at: http:// www.plim.org/Freemasonp1.htm) (accessed on August 10, 2010).

25. "The Masonic Founding of The United States of America," *Global Insights* (at: http:// www.nohoax.com/masonic_founding.htm) (accessed on August 10, 2010).

26. William Bramley, *The Gods of Eden* (New York: Avon Books, 1990), p. 279.

27. Albert Pike, *Morals and Dogma of the Ancient and Accepted Scottish Rite of Freemasonry* (Charleston, 1871), p. 524, Degree 26.

28. Manley P. Hall, *The Lost Keys of Freemasonry* (Canada: Philosophical Research Society, 1976), p. 65; See also, Newton, *Builders*, pp. 204-205: "Christianity in those days – as, alas, too often now – was another name for a petty and bigoted sectarianism; and Masonry by its very genius was, and is, unsectarian. . . . [T]he order itself is open to men of all faiths, Catholic and Protestant, Hebrew and Hindu, who confess faith in God; and so it will always remain."

29. Pike, *Morals and Dogma (1871)*, p. 223, Degree 14.

30. Pike, *Morals and Dogma (1871)*, p. 166, Digest of M & D.

31. Pike, *Morals and Dogma (1871)*, p. 660, Degree 28.

32. For example, "Sectarian of no creed, it [Scottish Rite Freemasonry] has yet thought it not improper to use the old allegories, based on occurrences detailed in the Hebrew and Christian books, and drawn from the Ancient Mysteries of Egypt, Persia, Greece, India, the Druids and the Essenes, as vehicles to communicate the Great Masonic Truths," from Pike, *Morals and Dogma*, p. 328; and "What the human thought of God is depends on what power of the mind or aspect of life man uses as a lens through which to look into the mystery of things. Conceived of as the will of the world, God is one, and we have the monotheism of Moses. Seen through instinct and the kaleidoscope of the senses, God is multiple, and the result is polytheism and its gods without number. For the reason, God is a dualism made up of matter and mind, as in the faith of Zoroaster and many other cults. But when the social life of man becomes the prism of faith, God is a trinity of Father, Mother, Child. Almost as old as human thought, we find the idea of the trinity and its triangle emblem everywhere – Siva, Vishnu, and Brahma in India corresponding to Osiris, Isis, and Horus in Egypt," from Newton, *Builders*, p. 20.

33. Pike, *Morals and Dogma*, p. 737, Degree 28.

34. Bishop Janes, *Mistakes of Ingersoll*, J. B. McClure, editor (Chicago: Rhodes & McClure, 1879), p. 259.

35. Carl H. Claudy, *Old Tiler Talks*, Cathedral Calendar, editor (Washington, D. C.: Fellowship Forum, 1925), p. 6; See also, Newton, *Builders*, pp. 204-205: "Christianity in those days – as, alas, too often now – was another name for a petty and bigoted sectarianism; and Masonry by its very genius was, and is, unsectarian. . . . [T]he order itself is open to men of all faiths, Catholic and Protestant, Hebrew and Hindu, who confess faith in God; and so it will always remain."

36. "What are America's True Roots?" *American Masonic History* (at: http://www.rapidnet. com/~jbeard/bdm/Psychology/mashist.htm) (accessed on August 10, 2010).

37. "What are America's True Roots?" *American Masonic History* (at: http://www.rapidnet. com/~jbeard/bdm/Psychology/mashist.htm) (accessed on August 10, 2010).

38. "Who are We?" *Masonic Service Association of North America* (at: http://www.msana. com) (accessed on August 10, 2010).

39. "Eye in the Pyramid" *Masonic Service Association of North America* (at: http://www. msana.com/stb_eyepyramid.htm) (accessed on August 10, 2010).

40. Sidney Morse, *Freemasonry In The American Revolution* (Washington, DC: Masonic Services Association, 1924), p. 44; See also Ronald E. Heaton, *Masonic Membership of the Founding Fathers* (Silver Spring, MD: Masonic Service Association, 1974), pp. 109-110.

41. Morse, *Freemasonry In The American Revolution*, p. 45.

42. Heaton, *Masonic Membership*, p. 109, quoting Oscar Jewell Harvey, *History of Lodge 61, F. & A. M., Wilkes-Barre, 1794-1897* (Wilkes-Barre, 1897), p. 82.

43. John Quincy Adams, *Letters on Freemasonry* (Hartford: Joseph Hurlbut, 1833), pp. 4-5, letter of August 22, 1831; See also John Quincy Adams, *Letters on the Masonic Institution* (Boston: T. R. Marvin, 1847), pp. 11-12, and *A Portrait of Masonry and Anti-masonry, As Drawn by Richard Rush, John Quincy Adams, William Wirt, etc.* (Providence: Office of the Daily Advertiser, 1832), pp. 56-58.

44. Heaton, *Masonic Membership*, p. 107.

45. James Madison, *Letters and Other Writings of James Madison, Fourth President of the United States* (New York: R. Worthington, 1884),Vol. IV, p. 150, letter to Stephen Bates, January 24, 1831.

46. Heaton, *Masonic Membership*, p. 91.

47. Heaton, *Masonic Membership*, p. 127.

48. "National Treasure," *Masonic Service Association of North America* (at: http://www. msana.com/micnatltreasure.htm) (accessed on August 10, 2010).

49. "Catholic Encyclopedia: Masonry (Freemasonry)," *New Advent* (at: http://www. newadvent.org/cathen/09771a.htm#VIII) (accessed on August 10, 2010).

50. Heaton, *Masonic Membership*, p. 134.

51. See the listing of non-Masonic Founding Fathers in Heaton, *Masonic Membership*, pp. 109-164.

52. Heaton, *Masonic Membership*, p. 16.

53. Heaton, *Masonic Membership*, p. 31.

54. Heaton, *Masonic Membership*, p. 43.

55. The Grand Lodge of Pennsylvania lists five signers of the Declaration as Free-masons (see Heaton, *Masonic Membership*, p. 93, quoting *GL Proc. Pennsylvania*, 1909, p. 463 – Report on Correspondence); while the Masonic Service Association lists nine signers of the Declaration as possible Freemasons (see Heaton, *Masonic Membership*, p. xvi). The maximum of nine Declaration signers who might have been Masons are John Hancock, Benjamin Franklin, William Hooper, William Whipple, Joseph Hewes, Robert Treat Paine, Richard Stockton, George Walton, and William Ellery; See also\ Freemasons & the U. S. Declaration of Independence," *Paul M. Bessel* (at: http://bessel. org/declmas.htm) (accessed on August 10, 2010).

56. Henry Wilson Coil, *Conversations on Freemasonry*, Lewis C. Wes Cook, editor (Chicago: Macok Publishing and Masonic Supply Co., 1976), pp. 265-266. Those delegates include George Washington, Benjamin Franklin, Edmund Randolph, John Blair, David

Brearley, Gunning Bedford, Jr., Oliver Ellsworth, Rufus King, John Dickinson, Jacob Broom, William Pierce, and Daniel Carroll. And according to Coil, six other delegates became Freemasons after the Convention: William Davie, Jr., James McHenry, John Mercer, William Patterson, Jonathan Dayton, and Daniel of St. Thomas Jenifer.

57. Thomas Jefferson, *The Works of Thomas Jefferson*, Paul Leicester Ford, editor (New York: G. P. Putnam's Sons, 1904), Vol. V, p. 332, letter to Joseph Jones, August 14, 1787.

58. See, for example, Alexander Hamilton: "Particular attachment to any foreign nation is an exotic sentiment which – where it exists – must derogate from [weaken] the affection due to our own country," *The Works of Alexander Hamilton*, John C. Hamilton, editor (New York: John F. Trow, 1851), Vol. V, p. 345; and George Washington: "Europe has a set of primary interests which to us have no – or a very remote – relation. . . . Why forego the advantages of [our] situation? Why quit [leave] our own to stand upon foreign ground?" *The Writings of George Washington*, Jared Sparks, editor (Boston: Ferdinand Andrews, 1838), Vol. XII, p. 231 Farewell Address, September 19, 1796.

59. See, for example, Salem Town, *A System of Speculative Masonry* (Salem, NY: Dodd and Stevenson, 1818); John Stearns, *An Inquiry into the Nature and Tendency of Speculative Free-Masonry* (Utica: Northway & Porter, 1829); Elder David Bernard, *Light on Masonry: A Collection of All the Most Important Documents on the Subject of Speculative Free Masonry* (Utica: William Williams, 1829).

60. Jewel P. Lightfoot, *Lightfoot's Manual of the Lodge* (Fort Worth: Masonic Home and School, 1934), p. 225.

61. William Morgan, *Illustrations of Masonry* (Batavia, NY, 1827), p. 25.

62. Morgan, *Illustrations*, p. 78.

63. *Portrait of Masonry*, pp. 43-45, William Wirt.

64. See the information available from the *Biographical Directory of the United States Congress* (at: http://bioguide.congress.gov/biosearch/biosearch.asp) (accessed on August 10, 2010).

65. "The Morgan Affair Aftermath," *Grand Lodge of British Columbia and Yukon* (at: http://freemasonry.bcy.ca./texts/MorganAffair.html) (accessed on August 10, 2010).

66. "The Morgan Affair Aftermath," *Grand Lodge of British Columbia and Yukon* (at: http://freemasonry.bcy.ca./texts/MorganAffair.html) (accessed on August 10, 2010).

67. "The Morgan Affair Aftermath," *Grand Lodge of British Columbia and Yukon* (at: http://freemasonry.bcy.ca./texts/MorganAffair.html) (accessed on August 10, 2010).

68. "The Morgan Affair Aftermath," *Grand Lodge of British Columbia and Yukon* (at: http://freemasonry.bcy.ca./texts/MorganAffair.html) (accessed on August 10, 2010).

69. "The Morgan Affair Aftermath," *Grand Lodge of British Columbia and Yukon* (at: http://freemasonry.bcy.ca./texts/MorganAffair.html) (accessed on August 10, 2010).

70. See, for example, Allen E. Roberts, *Freemasonry in American History* (Richmond, VA: Macoy Publishing, 1985), pp. 315, 223, 333, 325, 323, 379; "The Masonic Presidents Tour," *Grand Lodge of Pennsylvania* (at: http://www.pagrandlodge.org/mlam/presidents/index.html) (accessed on August 10, 2010).

71. See, for example, Roberts, *Freemasonry in American History*, p. 223.

72. See, for example, "Masonic Presidents of the United States," *Burbank Masonic Lodge No. 406* (at: http://www.calodges.org/no406/FAMASONS.HTM) (accessed on August 10, 2010).

73. "Letter of April 19, 1996, to U. S. Bishops by Cardinal Bernard Law," *Catholic*

Culture (at: http://www.catholicculture.org/docs/doc_view.cfm?recnum=5285) (accessed on August 10, 2010).

74. "Letter of April 19, 1996, to U. S. Bishops by Cardinal Bernard Law," *Catholic Culture* (at: http://www.catholicculture.org/docs/doc_view.cfm?recnum=5285) (accessed on August 10, 2010).

75. "History of Freemasonry," *Mastermason.com* (at: http://mastermason.com/rfire/masonry/history.html#Modern) (accessed on August 10, 2010).

76. According to information from the Southern Jurisdiction of Scottish Rite Freemasonry: "Membership in American Blue Lodges peaked in 1959, at:about 4,103,000, followed by over 40 years of decline to about 1,800,000 in 2002. The Scottish Rite (Northern and Southern Jurisdictions combined) has had 31 years of falling numbers since cresting in 1979 at 661,000" (at: http://www.srmason-sj.org/web/journal-files/Issues/aug02/morris.htm) (accessed on August 10, 2010). See also "Masonic Decline and Initiatic Tradition," *Freemasonry Today* (at: http://www.freemasonrytoday.com/issue29-article1.shtml) (accessed on August 10, 2010), and MSNBC, "Masons Among Us" (at: http://msnbc.msn.com/id/4500571) (accessed on August 10, 2010).

77. W. Smith, *Ahiman Rezon: Including A Sermon Preached in Christ-Church, Philadelphia [For the Benefit of the Poor] By Appointment of and Before the General Communication of Free and Accepted Masons of the State of Pennsylvania, On Monday, December 28, 1778* (Philadelphia: Hall and Sellers, 1783), pp. 159-160.

78. Shaw & McKenney, *Deadly Deception*, p. 76; A. G. Mackey, *Mackey's Masonic Ritualist* (New York: Clark & Maynard, 1879), p. 272.

79. William J. Walen, *Christianity and American Freemasonry* (Huntington, IN: Bruce Publishing Company, 1987), p. 53.

80. Walen, *Christianity and American Freemasonry*, p. 57.

81. McKenney, *Please Tell Me*, p. 37.

82. See numerous Masonic sources and websites, including "Why You, A Master Mason, Should be Interested in the York Rite of Freemasonry," *York Rite* (at: http://www.yorkrite.com/getrifold.html) (accessed on August 10, 2010); "Questions on York Rite and Its Degrees," *Mastermason.com* (at: http://www.mastermason.com/ocalayorkritebodies/body%20questions_on_york_rite.htm) (accessed on August 10, 2010); "What is York Rite Masonry?" *Grand Chapter of Royal Arch Masons of Alberta* (at: http://www.royalarchmasonsalberta.com/Welcome/YorkRite.htm) (accessed on August 10, 2010); "Purposes and Activities of the Knights Templar Organization," *Allen Web – York Rite Info Page* (at: http://members.aol.com/AllenWeb/yorkrite.html) (accessed on August 10, 2010); "The York Rite of Freemasonry," *Freemasonry 101* (at: http://www.tracingboard.com/york_rite.htm) (accessed on August 10, 2010); "York Rite Honorary Bodies," *York Rite Allied & Appendant Bodies* (at :http://www.geocities.com/Athens/Forum/6255/Allied.html) (accessed on August 10, 2010); *Indexed Bible* [Masonic Edition], p. 10; and numerous other sources.

83. McKenney, *Please Tell Me*, pp. 103-104, quoting Harmon R. Taylor, *Oil and Water* (Newtonville, NY: HRT Ministries, undated pamphlet), from a personal interview at Knoxville, TN, on June 5, 1993.

84. Charles Brockwell, *Brotherly Love Recommended in a Sermon Preached Before the Ancient and Honorable Society of Free and Accepted Masons, in Christ Church, Boston, on Wednesday the 27th of December, 1749* (Boston: John Draper, 1749), p. 14.

85. Wellins Calcott, *A Candid Disquisition of the Principles and Practices of the Most Ancient and Honorable Society of Free and Accepted Masons* (London: William M'Alpine, 1771), p. 169.

86. Albert G. Mackey, *History of Freemasonry* (New York: The Masonic History Co.,

1898), Vol. I, p. 136.

87. Town, *System of Speculative Masonry*, p. 14.

88. Town, *System of Speculative Masonry*, p. 49.

89. For example: "The Bible is used among Masons as a symbol of the will of God, however it may be expressed. And, therefore, whatever to any people expresses that will may be used as a substitute for the Bible in a Masonic Lodge. Thus, in a Lodge consisting entirely of Jews, the Old Testament alone may be placed upon the altar, and Turkish Masons make use of the Koran. Whether it be the Gospels to the Christian, the Pentateuch to the Israelite, the Koran to the Mussulman, or the Vedas to the Brahman, it everywhere Masonically conveys the same idea – that of the symbolism of the Divine Will revealed to man," from Mackey, *Encyclopedia*, Vol. 1, p. 104; and "The Bible is an indispensable part of the furniture of the Christian Lodge, only because it is the sacred book of the Christian religion. The Hebrew Pentateuch in a Hebrew Lodge, and the Koran in a Mohammedan one, belong on the Altar; and one of these, and the Square and Compass, properly understood, are the Great Lights by which a Mason must walk and work," Pike, *Morals and Dogma*, p. 11.

90. Town, *System of Speculative Masonry*, p. 37.

91. *Dictionary of American Biography*, s.v. "DeWitt Clinton"; and *Sixth Report of the American Bible Society, May 9, 1822* (New York: Daniel Fanshaw, 1822), "Officers of the American Bible Society."

92. For example: "[The Bible's] extensive circulation is a duty of the most imperative nature, and an interest of the highest character" and "Jesus Christ appeared, pointing out the way to heaven, and shedding light over the world." William Campbell, *The Life and Writings of DeWitt Clinton* (New York: Baker and Scribner, 1849), pp. 299, 304.

93. *Appleton's Cyclopedia of American Biography*, s.v. "William Smith."

94. *Dictionary of American Biography*, s.v. "William Smith."

95. Smith, *Ahiman Rezon* (Philadelphia: Hall and Sellers, 1783), pp. 109, 111-112.

96. Smith, *Ahiman Rezon*, p. 163.

97. *Dictionary of American Biography*, s.v. "William White."

98. *Colonial Freemasonry*, Louis C. Wes Cook, editor (Transactions of the Missouri Lodge of Research, 1973-1974), Vol. 30, p. 10.

99. Reverend William Walter, *A Charge Delivered at Charlestown, to the Worshipful Master, the Wardens and Brethren of King Solomon's Lodge, on the Festival of St. John the Baptist 1793*, pp. 28-30, published with Josiah Bartlett's *Discourse on the Origin, Progress, and Design of Freemasonry* (Boston: Brother Thomas and John Fleet, 1793).

100. Rev. Thaddeus Mason Harris, *A Discourse Delivered at the Public Consecration of the Meridian Sun Lodge* (Brookfield, MA: E. Merriam and Co., 1798), p. 7.

101. Albert G. Mackey, *History of Freemasonry in South Carolina* (1861), pp. 15-20, quoted from Mackey, *Encyclopedia*, Vol. II, p. 680.

102. Mackey, *Encyclopedia*, Vol. II, p. 680.

103. Steven C. Bullock, *Revolutionary Brotherhood* (Chapel Hill: University of North Carolina Press, 1996), p. 171.

104. Bullock, *Revolutionary Brotherhood*, p. 163.

105. Thomas Paine, *The Writings of Thomas Paine*, Moncure Daniel Conway, editor (New York: G. P. Putnam's Sons, 1896), Vol. IV, p. 293.

106. Paine, *Writings* (1896), Vol. IV, pp. 293-94.

107. *Dictionary of American Biography*, s.v. "Ezra Stiles."

108. Ezra Stiles, *The Literary Diary of Ezra Stiles,* Franklin Bowditch Dexter, editor (New York: Charles Scribner's Sons, 1901), Vol. I, p. 56.

109. Bullock, *Revolutionary Brotherhood,* p. 51.

110. Bullock, *Revolutionary Brotherhood,* p. 176.

111. Bullock, *Revolutionary Brotherhood,* p. 164; see also Mackey, *Encyclopedia,* Vol. I, p. 439.

112. Robert Morey, *The Truth About Masons* (Eugene, OR: Harvest House, 1993).

113. Morey, *Truth About Masons,* p. 30.

114. Jim Shaw & Tom C. McKenney, *The Deadly Deception* (Louisiana: Huntington House, 1988).

115. McKenney, *Please Tell Me,* p. 164.

116. *Americanized Encyclopedia Britannica* (1890), s.v. "Freemasonry."

117. Roberts, *Freemasonry in American History,* p. 85.

118. According to Mackey, the first attempt to de-Christianize the Craft was in 1813, and although the Fraternity largely rejected that initial attempt, a shift nevertheless slowly began. Mackey, *History,* p. 137.

119. For example, the 1820 Pittsburgh Presbyterian Synod criticized Freemasonry for "embrac[ing] with equal affection the Pagan, the Deist, the Turk and the Christian," and condemned the system as "opposed to the doctrines and aims of the gospel of Christ." *Proceedings of the Centennial Celebration of the Presbyterian Church of Greensburg, Pennsylvania, . . . 1888* (Greensburg, PA, 1888), p. 50.

120. See, for example, Paul Fisher, *Behind the Lodge Door* (Rockford, IL: Tan Books and Publishers, 1994), pp. 237-240; Stephen Knight, *The Brotherhood* (London: Grafton Books, 1983), p. 317; J. Edward Decker, *The Question of Freemasonry* (Lafayette, LA: Huntington House, 1992), p. 27; McKenney, *Please Tell Me,* pp. 33-34, 147-149.

121. William Morgan, *The Mysteries of Freemasonry; Containing All the Degrees of the Order Conferred in a Mason's Lodge,* George R. Crafts, editor (New York: Wilson & Co., 1827), p. 6; see also Avery Allyn, *A Ritual of Freemasonry* (New York: L. Fitzgerald, 1831), p. 34.

122. Morgan, *Mysteries of Freemasonry,* p. 6; see also Allyn, *Ritual of Freemasonry,* p. 35.

123. Morgan, *Mysteries of Freemasonry,* p. 16; see also Allyn, *Ritual of Freemasonry,* p. 60.

124. Morgan, *Mysteries of Freemasonry,* p. 23; see also Allyn, *Ritual of Freemasonry,* p. 71.

125. A. T. C. Pierson and Godfrey W. Steinbrenner, *The Traditions, Origins and Early History of Freemasonry* (New York: Masonic Publishing Co., 1885), pp. 145-146.

126. *Portrait of Masonry,* p. 45, William Wirt.

127. "Freemasonry Around the World," *Saints Alive* (at: http://www.saintsalive.com/freemasonry/fmworld.htm) (accessed on August 10, 2010).

128. John Robison, *Proofs of a Conspiracy Against all the Religions and Governments of Europe, Carried on in the Secret Meetings of Free Masons, Illuminati, and Reading Societies* (Philadelphia: T. Dobson, 1798), pp. 60-61.

129. Jedediah Morse, *A Sermon Delivered at the New North Church in Boston . . . May 9th, 1798, Being the Day Recommended by John Adams, President of the United States of America, for Solemn Humiliation, Fasting and Prayer* (Boston: Samuel Hall, 1798).

130. David Tappan, *A Discourse Delivered in the Chapel of Harvard College, June 19, 1798* (Boston, 1798).

131. Timothy Dwight, *The Duty of Americans, at the Present Crisis . . . Fourth of July, 1798* (New Haven, CT, 1798).

132. Jedediah Morse, *A Sermon Preached at Charlestown, November 29, 1798, on the An-*

niversary Thanksgiving in Massachusetts. With an Appendix, Designed to Illustrate Some Parts of the Discourse; Exhibiting Proofs of the Early Existence, Progress, and Deleterious Effects of French Intrigue and Influence in the United States (Boston: Samuel Hall, 1799).

133. Morse, *Sermon Preached at Charlestown*, pp. 22-23.

134. See "Jedediah Morse and the Illuminati," *Grand Lodge of British Columbia and Yukon* (at: http://freemasonry.bcy.ca/anti-masonry/morse.html) (accessed on August 10, 2010).

135. Jedediah Morse, *A Sermon Exhibiting the Present Dangers and Consequent Duties of the Citizens of the United States of America. Delivered at Charlestown, April 25, 1799, the Day of the National Fast* (Hartford: Hudson and Goodwin, 1799).

136. See "Jedediah Morse and the Illuminati," *Grand Lodge of British Columbia and Yukon* (at: http://freemasonry.bcy.ca/anti-masonry/morse.html) (accessed on August 10, 2010).

137. Thomas Jefferson, *The Papers of Thomas Jefferson,* Barbara Oberg, editor (Princeton: Princeton University Press, 2004), Vol. 31, p. 350, letter to Bishop James Madison, January 31, 1800.

138. Jefferson, *Papers* (2004), Vol. 31, p. 350, letter to Bishop James Madison, January 31, 1800.

139. Jedediah Morse, *A Sermon Delivered Before the Grand Lodge of Free & Accepted Masons of the Commonwealth of Massachusetts, at a Public Installation of the Officers of the Corinthian Lodge, at Concord, in the County of Middlesex, June 25th, 1798* (Leominster, MA: Charles, & John Prentiss, 1798).

140. Morse, *Sermon Delivered Before the Grand Lodge* (1798) , p. 19.

141. George Washington, *The Papers of George Washington,* W. W. Abbot, editor (Charlottesville: University Press of Virginia, 1998), Vol. 2, p. 554, letter from G. W. Snyder, August 22, 1798.

142. Washington, *Papers* (1998), Vol. 2, p. 555, letter to G. W. Snyder, September 25, 1798.

143. George Washington, *The Writings of George Washington from the Original Manuscript Sources, 1745-1799,* John C. Fitzpatrick, editor (Washington: Government Printing Office, 1940), Vol. 33, pp. 475-476, letter to Henry Lee, August 26, 1794.

144. Washington, *Writings* (1940), Vol. 34, p. 17, letter to John Jay, November 1, 1794.

145. Washington, *Writings* (1940), Vol. 33, p. 506, letter to Burgess Ball, September 25, 1794.

146. Washington, *Papers* (1998), Vol. 2, pp. 555-556, letter from G. W. Snyder, October 1, 1798.

147. Washington, *Papers* (1998), Vol. 2, p. 556, letter from G. W. Snyder, October 1, 1798.

148. Washington, *Papers* (1998), Vol. 2, p. 557, letter to G. W. Snyder, October 24, 1798.

149. The Rev. Abraham Clarke, *The Secrets of Masonry Illustrated and Explained; in a Discourse, Preached at South-Kingston, Before the Grand Lodge of this State of Rhode Island* (Providence: Bennett Wheeler, 1799), pp. 12-13.

150. Jefferson, *Papers* (2004), Vol. 31, p. 350, letter to Bishop James Madison, January 31, 1800.

151. Clarke, *Secrets of Masonry*, pp. 1, 12-13.

152. "The French Revolution," *Penglais School – History Department* (at: http://www.penglais.ceredigion.sch.uk/history/hsyden.html) (accessed on August 10, 2010).

153. Noah Webster, *The Revolution in France Considered in Respect to Its Progress and Effects* (New York: George Bunce, 1794), p. 20.

154. Webster, *Revolution in France,* (1794) p. 20.

155. George Washington, *Address of George Washington. . . Preparatory to His Declination* (Baltimore:George & Henry S. Keatinge, 1796), pp. 22-23.

156. Washington, *Writings* (1941), Vol. 36, p. 453, letter to G. W. Snyder, September 25, 1798.

157. William A. Brown, *When & Where: A Chronology of the Life of George Washington* (United States: William A. Brown, 1984).

158. In the early years of American Freemasonry, most lodges confined the awarding of degrees to the first three. A few independent Masonic entities occasionally conferred additional degrees, but this was relatively rare and such conferrals generally occurred in widely separated locations. In 1801, those separate entities were consolidated into the Scottish Rite, where their higher degrees were standardized. See, for example, Pierson and Steinbrenner, *Traditions, Origins and Early History*, p. 321, 327, 138-139; Melvin M. Johnson, *Beginnings of Freemasonry in America* (New York: George H. Doran Company, 1924), p. 22.

159. See, for example, Clarke, *Secrets of Masonry*, (1799), p. 13.

160. Washington, *Writings* (1941), Vol. 36, pp. 452-453, letter to G. W. Snyder, September 25, 1798.

161. Washington Lodge (Military) on October 6, 1779; Lodge No. 9 (Yorktown) on October 22, 1781; Solomon's Lodge No. 1 (Poughkeepsie, NY) on December 27, 1782; and Alexandria Lodge 39 (VA) on June 24, 1784.

162. William Allen, *In The Greatest Solemn Dignity: The Capitol's Four Cornerstones* (Washington: Government Printing Office, 1994), p. 7, "Washington Laying the Cornerstone of the Capitol, 1793," mural by Allyn Cox.

163. McKenney, *Please Tell Me*, (1994), p. 162.

164. See Washington's explanation of his refusal in *Writings* (1932), Vol. 32, pp. 83-84, letter to Henry Lee July 3, 1792.

165. Arnoldo Editore, *The Life & Times of Washington* (Philadelphia: Curtis Books, 1967), p. 13.

166. Michael Baigent and Richard Leigh, *The Temple and the Lodge* (New York: Arcade Publishing, 1989), p. 253, citing Milborne, "British Military Lodges in the American War of Independence," p. 50.

167. Baigent and Leigh, *Temple and the Lodge*, p. 253, citing Milborne, "British Military Lodges in the American War of Independence," pp. 50, 67.

168. Baigent and Leigh, *Temple and the Lodge* (1989), p. 203.

169. Baigent and Leigh, *Temple and the Lodge* (1989), pp. 206-207.

170. Morse, *Freemasonry In The American Revolution*, p. 74.

171. Morse, *Freemasonry In The American Revolution*, pp. 16-17.

172. Washington, *Writings* (1931), Vol. I, p. 22, n45; Brown, *When & Where*, p. 7.

173. Baigent and Leigh, *Temple and the Lodge* (1989), p. 211, citing Heaton, *Masonic Membership* and Denslow, *10,000 Famous Freemasons;* see also *Colonial Freemasonry*, Vol. 30, p. 194, James R. Case, "American Union Lodge."

174. J. Hugo Tatsch, *Freemasonry in the Thirteen Colonies* (New York: Macoy Publishing and Masonic Supply Company, 1929), p. 181.

175. Tatsch, *Freemasonry in the Thirteen Colonies*, p. 203; see also Sidney Hayden, *Washington and his Masonic Compeers* (New York: Masonic Publishing and Manufacturing Co., 1868), pp. 73-75; and Peters, *Masons As Makers*, p. 5.

176. Morse, *Freemasonry In The American Revolution*, p. 131.

177. Thomas Egleston, *The Life of John Paterson, Major-General in the Revolutionary Army* (New York: G. P. Putnam's Sons, 1898), p. 201.

178. "The Masonic New World Order," *Watch Unto Prayer* (at: http://watch.pair.com/mason.html) (accessed on August 10, 2010); see also "Masonic Symbols of Power in Their

Seat of Power," *Cutting Edge Ministries* (at: http://www.cuttingedge.org/news/n1040.html) (accessed on August 10, 2010).

179. Tim Bryce, "An Introduction to Freemasonry" (at: http://www.os2ss.com/connect/masons/present.htm) (accessed on August 10, 2010).

180. Decker, *Question of Freemasonry*, p. 33.

181. "Freemasonry – Is it satan's Door to America?" *Saints Alive* (at: http://www.saintsalive.com/freemasonry/fmsatansdoor.html) (accessed on August 10, 2010).

182. "Freemasonry – Is it satan's Door to America?" *Saints Alive* (at: http://www.saintsalive.com/freemasonry/fmsatansdoor.html) (accessed on August 10, 2010).

183. "Thomas Jefferson Memorial: Physical History," *National Park Service* (at: http://www.nps.gov/thje/cli/cli_history_parta.pdf) (accessed on August 10, 2010).

184. "The Masonic New World Order," *Watch Unto Prayer* (at: http://watch.pair.com/mason.html) (accessed on August 10, 2010).

185. "Freemasonry – Is it satan's Door to America?" *Saints Alive* (at: http://www.saintsalive.com/freemasonry/fmsatansdoor.html) (accessed on August 10, 2010).

186. Baigent and Leigh, *Temple and the Lodge*, p. 262.

187. J. R. Church, *Guardians of the Grail* (Oklahoma City: Prophecy Publications, 1989), pp. 164-165.

188. "Cutting Edge Book Review: America's Secret Destiny," *Cutting Edge Ministries* (at: http://www.cuttingedge.org/review/rv143.html) (accessed on August 10, 2010).

189. Church, *Guardians*, pp. 147-148.

190. Biagent and Leigh, *Temple and the Lodge*, p. 261.

191. *Journals of the Continental Congress, 1774-1789* (Washington: Government Printing Office, 1906), Vol. 5, pp. 517-518, July 4, 1776.

192. "Freemasonry and Secret Societies," *PLIM Report* (at: http://www.plim.org/Freemasonp1.htm) (accessed on August 10, 2010).

193. "New World Order: Symbol of the Illuminati," *Lifeline Back to the Bible* (at: http://www.jesus-is-lord.co.za/Lifeline/NewWorldOrder.htm) (accessed on August 10, 2010).

194. John Adams, *Letters of John Adams, Addressed to His Wife*, Charles Francis Adams, editor (Boston: Charles C. Little and James Brown, 1841), Vol. I, p. 152, letter to Abigail Adams, August 14, 1776.

195. Adams, *Letters* (1841), Vol. I, p. 152, letter to Abigail Adams, August 14, 1776.

196. *Journals* (1906), Vol. 5, pp. 689-690, August 20, 1776.

197. See "The Great Seal of the United States," *U. S. Department of State* (at: http://www.state.gov/documents/organization/27807.pdf) (accessed on August 10, 2010).

198. Richard S. Patterson and Richardson Dougall, *The Eagle and the Shield* (Washington: Department of State, 1976), pp. 32-33.

199. Patterson and Dougall, *Eagle and the Shield* (1976), p. 44.

200. Patterson and Dougall, *Eagle and the Shield* (1976), p. 71.

201. *Journals* (1914), Vol. 22, pp. 338-340; see also B. J. Cigrand, *Story of the Great Seal of the United States* (Chicago: Cameron, Amberg & Co., 1892), pp. 220-225.

202. Jim Marrs, *Rule by Secrecy: The Hidden History That Connects the Trilateral Commission, the Freemasons, and the Great Pyramids* (New York: HarperCollins, 2000), p. 235.

203. "New World Order: Symbol of the Illuminati," *Lifeline Back to the Bible* (at: http://www.jesus-is-lord.co.za/Lifeline/NewWorldOrder.htm) (accessed on August 10, 2010); "Final Warning: A History of the New World Order," *The Seventh Fire* (at: http://www.

the7thfire.com/new world order/final warning/final warning table of contents.htm) (accessed on August 10, 2010).

204. For example, Ronald E. Heaton, *Masonic Membership of the Founding Fathers* (Silver Spring: Masonic Service Association, 1974), lists the Founders who are Masons; he does not list Thomson as a Mason – nor do other Masonic writers.

205. Patterson and Dougall, *Eagle and the Shield*, p. 85.

206. James Madison, *The Papers of James Madison*, Henry D. Gilpin, editor (Washington: Langtree and O'Sullivan, 1840), Vol. II, pp. 984-985, June 28, 1787.

207. Samuel Adams, *By the Governor. A Proclamation for a Day of Public Fasting, Humiliation, and Prayer* (Massachusetts: Adams and Larkin, 1795), February 28, 1795.

208. Alexander Hamilton, John Jay, & James Madison, *The Federalist* (Philadelphia: Benjamin Warner, 1818), p. 194, James Madison, Federalist #38; see also Federalist #2 (p. 12) and Federalist #20 (p. 105) for other acknowledgments of the blessings of Providence upon America.

209. Washington, *Writings* (1838), Vol. VI, p. 36, letter to Brigadier General Nelson, August 20, 1778.

210. For examples of ministers who used both clear evangelical terms as well as what today are errantly considered "deistic" descriptions for God, see Samuel Stanhope Smith, *The Divine Goodness to the United States of America – A Discourse on the Subjects of National Gratitude* (Philadelphia: William Young, 1795); Jonathan French, *A Sermon Delivered on the Anniversary of Thanksgiving, November 29, 1798* (Andover: Ames and Parker, 1799); Rev. Joseph Willard, *A Thanksgiving Sermon Delivered at Boston December 11, 1783* (Boston: T. and J. Fleet, 1784); William Hazlitt, *A Thanksgiving Sermon Preached at Hallowell, December 15, 1785* (Boston: Samuel Hall, 1786); Evan Johns, *The Happiness of American Christians, A Thanksgiving Sermon Preached on Thursday the 24th of November 1803* (Hartford: Hudson and Goodwin, 1804); Isaac Backus, *An Appeal to the Public for Religious Liberty* (Boston: John Boyle, 1783); *et. al.*

211. *The Constitutions of the Several Independent States of America* (Boston: Norman and Bowen, 1785), p. 81, Pennsylvania, 1776, Chapter II, Section 10.

212. See, for example, *The Constitutions of the Sixteen States* (Boston: Manning and Loring, 1797), p. 257, Vermont, 1792, Chapter II, Section XII; and *Constitutions* (1797), p. 274, Tennessee, 1796, Article VIII, Section II; and *Constitutions* (1785), p. 146, South Carolina, 1776, Section 13.

213. "Eye in the Pyramid," *Masonic Service Association of North America* (at: http://www.msana.com/stb eyepyramid.htm) (accessed on August 10, 2010).

214. "Eye in the Pyramid," *Masonic Service Association of North America* (at: http://www.msana.com/stb eyepyramid.htm) (accessed on August 10, 2010).

215. "Eye in the Pyramid," *Masonic Service Association of North America* (at: http://www.msana.com/stb eyepyramid.htm) (accessed on August 10, 2010).

216. Heaton, *Masonic Membership*, p. 131.

217. George Hastings, *The Life and Works of Francis Hopkinson* (Chicago: University of Chicago Press, 1926), pp. 75-79, 366.

218. Hastings, *Life and Works* (1926), p. 71.

219. See, for example, Francis Hopkinson, *Life and Works of Francis Hopkinson*, George Everett Hastings, editor (Chicago: University of Chicago Press, 1926), pp. 179-180; see also Francis Hopkinson, *The Miscellaneous Essays and Occasional Writings of Francis Hopkinson* (Philadelphia: T. Dobson, 1792), Vol. III, pp. 65-69, 104-106, 118-119 *et. al.*

220. Patterson and Dougall, *Eagle and the Shield*, p. 34.

221. Patterson and Dougall, *Eagle and the Shield*, pp. 34, 42.

222. Patterson and Dougall, *Eagle and the Shield*, pp. 35-37.

223. Patterson and Dougall, *Eagle and the Shield*, p. 66, illustration 11.

224. *Journals* (1914), Vol. 22, p. 339.

225. "Eye in the Pyramid," *Masonic Service Association of North America* (at: http://www. msana.com/stb_eyepyramid.htm) (accessed on August 10, 2010).

226. "FAQs: Currency," *United States Department of the Treasury* (at: http://www.treas. gov/education/faq/currency/portraits.shtml) (accessed on August 10, 2010).

227. Typical of the many claims is this one: "The motto inscribed beneath the pyramid in the Great Seal of America is 'Novus Ordo Seclorum' which is Latin for 'New Order of the Ages,' and synonymous with the 'New World Order'" from "The NWO, Freemasonry, & Symbols on the Dollar Bill," *World Newsstand* (at: http://www.wealth4freedom.com/ dollarbill.html) (accessed on August 10, 2010); there are many other examples.

228. *Journals* (1914), Vol. 22, p. 340.

229. Henry Clausen, *Masons Who Helped Shape our Nation* (San Diego: Neyenesch Printers, 1976), p. 82.

230. See, for example, E. C. Wines, *Commentaries on the Laws of the Ancient Hebrews* (New York: Geo. P. Putnam & Co., 1855), p. 490 [This work has been contemporarily reprinted as E. C. Wines, *The Roots of the American Republic* (Plymouth: Plymouth Rock Foundation, 1997)] in which Wines explains, "Each of the Israelitish tribes formed a separate state, having a local legislature and a distinct administration of justice. The power of the several states was sovereign within the limits of their reserved rights. Still, there was both a real and a vigorous general government. The nation might have been styled the united tribes, provinces, or states of Israel. The bond of political union between the sovereign states appears to have been fourfold. In other words, there were four departments of the Hebrew government: viz. the chief magistrate, whether judge, high priest, or king; the senate of princes; the congregation of Israel, the popular branch of the government; and the oracle of Jehovah, a most interesting and singular part of the political structure." The American government paralleled this federal system with the exception of the fourth characteristic: "the oracle of Jehovah."

231. "Eye in the Pyramid," *Masonic Service Association of North America* (at: http://www. msana.com/stb_eyepyramid.htm) (accessed on August 10, 2010).

232. Church, *Guardians*, pp. 152-153.

233. Church, *Guardians*, pp. 145-146.

234. Morey, *Truth About Masons*, p. 64.

235. Allen Trelease, *White Terror: The Ku Klux Klan Conspiracy and Southern Reconstruction* (New York: Harper & Row, 1971), pp. 20-21; Stanley Horn, *Invisible Empire: The Story of the Ku Klux Klan 1866-1871* (New York: Gordon Press, 1972), pp. 245, 337; J. C. Lester and D. L. Wilson, *Ku Klux Klan: Its Origin, Growth and Disbandment* (St. Clair Shores, MI: Scholarly Press, 1972), pp. 19, 27.

236. Pike, *Morals and Dogma* (1871), pp. 328, 275, 369-370, 103, 617-618.

237. Arthur Edward Waite, *A New Encyclopedia of Freemasonry* (New York: Weathervane Books, 1970), Vol. 2, p. 278.

238. Waite, *New Encyclopedia* (1970), Vol. 2, p. 278, quoting Dr. Fort Newton (1880-1950), a state Lodge official in Iowa and a Masonic author.

239. Waite, *New Encyclopedia* (1970), Vol. 2, p. 278.

240. Alphonse Cerza, *Anti-Masonry* (Fulton, MO: Ovid Bell Press, 1962), p. 255, Albert Pike, "Allocution of the Grand Commander."

241. Heaton, *Masonic Membership*, p. 25.

242. *Constitutions* (1785), p. 31, Massachusetts, 1780, Chapter VI, Article 1.

243. *Independent Chronicle* (Boston), November 2, 1780, last page; see also Abram English Brown, *John Hancock, His Book* (Boston: Lee and Shepard, 1898), p. 269.

244. *Independent Chronicle* (Boston), November 2, 1780, last page; see also Brown, *John Hancock* (1898), p. 269.

245. John Hancock, *By His Excellency John Hancock, Esq.; Governor and Commander in Chief in and Over the Commonwealth of Massachusetts. A Proclamation, For a Day of Thanksgiving* (Boston, 1780), for November 8, 1780; from an original broadside in possession of the author.

246. John Hancock, *A Proclamation for a Day of Fasting, Humiliation and Prayer* (Boston, 1782), for April 11, 1782; from an original broadside in possession of the author.

247. John Hancock, *By His Excellency John Hancock, Esq.; Governor of the Commonwealth of Massachusetts. A Proclamation, For a Day of Public Fasting and Prayer* (Boston, 1783), for April 23, 1783; from an original broadside in possession of the author.

248. Hancock, *Proclamation*, for April 23, 1783; from an original broadside in possession of the author.

249. John Hancock, *By His Excellency John Hancock, Esquire, Governor of the Commonwealth of Massachusetts. A Proclamation, For a Day of Public Thanksgiving* (Boston, 1790), for September 16, 1790; published in Columbian Centinel (Boston: 1790), p. 3.

250. John Hancock, *By His Excellency John Hancock, Esq. Governor of the Commonwealth of Massachusetts. A Proclamation, For a Day of Public Thanksgiving* (Boston, 1791), for October 15, 1791; published in Columbian Centinel (Boston: 1791), P. 1.

251. Heaton, *Masonic Membership*, p. 64.

252. Will of Richard Stockton, May 20, 1780; copies of these wills are in the files of the author; they may be obtained from various state archives and historical societies.

253. Heaton, *Masonic Membership*, p. 15.

254. John Dickinson, *The Political Writings of John Dickinson, Esquire, Late President of the United States of Delaware, and of the Commonwealth of Pennsylvania* (Wilmington: Bonsal and Niles, 1801), Vol. I, pp. 111-112.

255. John Dickinson, *The Writings of John Dickinson*, Paul Leicester Ford, editor (Philadelphia: Historical Society of Pennsylvania, 1895), Vol. I, p. 496, from Letter IV, "To the Inhabitants of the British Colonies in America."

256. Will of John Dickinson, March 7, 1808.

257. Heaton, *Masonic Membership*, p. 48.

258. Robert Treat Paine, *The Papers of Robert Treat Paine*, Stephen Riley and Edward Hanson, editors (Boston: Massachusetts Historical Society, 1992), Vol. I, p. 49.

259. Robert Treat Paine, *Papers* (1992), Vol. I, p. 300.

260. Will of Robert Treat Paine, May 11, 1814.

261. Heaton, *Masonic Membership*, pp. 42-43; *Colonial Freemasonry*, pp. 213-214, Alphonse Cerza, "Our Founding Fathers."

262. Bernard C. Steiner, *One Hundred and Ten Years Of Bible Society Work in Maryland: 1810-1920* (Baltimore: Maryland Bible Society, 1921), pp. 10-12.

263. Steiner, *Bible Society Work* (1921), p. 14.

264. Heaton, *Masonic Membership*, p. 4; *Colonial Freemasonry*, p. 213, Alphonse Cerza, "Our Founding Fathers."

265. Gunning Bedford, *Funeral Oration, upon the Death of General George Washington. Prepared at the Request of the Masonic Lodge, No. 14, of Wilmington ... and Delivered on St. John the Evangelist's Day ... and Now Published at the Particular Desire of the Lodge* (Wilmington: James Wilson, 1800), p. 15.

266. Bedford, *Funeral Oration* (1800), p. 18.

267. See, for example, "United States Presidents and The Masonic Power Structure," *Wake Up America* (at: http://www.heart7.net/uspresidentasmasons.htm) (accessed on August 10, 2010); "Mountain View Lodge No. 194: A Basic Masonic Education Course," *California Masonic Lodges* (at: http://www.calodges.org/no194/Masonic_Education.htm) (accessed on August 10, 2010); etc.

268. William J. Peterson, *A Brief History of the American Sunday School Union* (American Sunday School Union, 1969), p. 6; see also *Dictionary of American Biography*, s.v. "Francis Scott Key."

269. Henry Dwight, *The Centennial History of the American Bible Society* (New York: MacMillan Company, 1916), p. 73.

270. Hugh A. Garland, *The Life of John Randolph of Roanoke* (New York: D. Appleton & Company, 1853), Vol. II, p. 102, letter to Dr. Brockenbrough, September 25, 1818.

271. Garland, *Life of John Randolph* (1853), Vol. II, pp. 67-68, letter to Francis Scott Key.

272. Garland, *Life of John Randolph* (1853), Vol. II, pp. 99-100, letter to Francis Scott Key, September 7, 1818.

273. Garland, *Life of John Randolph* (1853), Vol. II, p. 104, letter from Francis Scott Key.

274. Benjamin Franklin, *The Works of Benjamin Franklin*, Jared Sparks, editor (Boston: Tappan, Whittemore, and Mason, 1840), Vol. X, pp. 281-282.

275. Adams, *Letters* (1841), Vol. I, p. 152, letter to Abigail Adams, August 14, 1776.

276. Benjamin Franklin, *The Papers of Benjamin Franklin* (New Haven: Yale University Press, 1961), Vol. 3, pp. 226-227, n, *Proclamation for a General Fast on December 9, 1747*, written by Franklin; see also Franklin, *Works* (1840), Vol. I, pp. 148-149.

277. Jared Sparks, *Life of Benjamin Franklin* (Boston: Tappan and Dennet, 1844), p. 352; see also Franklin, *Works* (1840), Vol. X, pp. 208- 209, n, letter to Granville Sharp, July 5, 1785.

278. Franklin, *Papers* (1963), Vol. 6, p. 469, letter to George Whitefield, July 2, 1756.

279. See, for example, Franklin, *Papers* (1972), Vol. 15, p. 30, letter to Francis Hopkinson, January 24, 1768, and Vol. 14, p. 340, letter to Francis Hopkinson, December 16, 1767.

280. See, for example, Franklin, *Papers* (1963), Vol. 7, pp. 100-101, letter from John Waring, January 24, 1757; p. 356, letter to John Waring, January 3, 1758; pp. 377-378, letter to John Waring, February 17, 1758; Vol. 9, pp. 12-13, letter from John Waring, January 4, 1760, also n1; pp. 20-21, "Minutes of the Associates of the Late Dr. Bray," January 17, 1760; Vol. 10, pp. 298-300, letter to John Waring, June 27, 1763; pp. 395-396, letter to John Waring, December 17, 1763; Vol. 13, p. 442, letter to Abbot Upcher, October 4, 1766; and others.

281. Benjamin Franklin, *Proposals Relating to the Education of Youth in Pennsylvania* (Philadelphia: University of Pennsylvania Press, 1931 reprint of 1749), p. vii, from the Introduction.

282. Franklin, *Proposals* (1749, 1931), p. 22.

283. James Madison, *The Papers of James Madison*, Henry D. Gilpin, editor (Washington: Langtree and O'Sullivan, 1840), Vol. II, pp. 984-986, Franklin's speech of June 28, 1787.

284. Benjamin Franklin, *Works of the Late Doctor Benjamin Franklin* (Dublin: P. Wogan,

P. Byrne, J. More, and W. Janes, 1793), p. 149.

285. Franklin, [Sparks] *Works* (1840), Vol. X, p. 422, letter from Ezra Stiles, January 28, 1790.

286. Franklin, [Sparks] *Works* (1840), Vol. X, p. 422, letter to Ezra Stiles, March 9, 1790.

287. Franklin, [Sparks] *Works* (1840), Vol. X, pp. 421-425, letter to Ezra Stiles, March 9, 1790.

288. OLIVER ELLSWORTH: *The Connecticut Courant* (Hartford), June 7, 1802, p. 3, "A Report of the Committee...to the General Assembly of the State of Connecticut;" JACOB BROOM: See, for example, his letter to his son, James, on February 24, 1794 (the original is in the possession of the author), wherein he says "[D]on't forget to be a Christian. I have said much to you on this head and I hope an indelible impression is made" (at: http://www. wallbuilders.com/LIBissuesArticles.asp?id=52); WILLIAM ELLORY: Jared Sparks, *Lives of William Pinkney, William Ellery,* and *Cotton Mather* (New York Harper and Brothers, 1856), from *The Library of American Biography,* Vol. VI, pp. 135-136 (at: http://books.google.com/books?id=9NgDAAAAYAAJ&printsec=fontcover&source=gbs_ge_summary_r&cad=onepage&q&f=false) ; and others.

289. George Washington, *Maxims of Washington; Political, Social, Moral and Religious,* John F. Schroeder, editor (New York: D. Appleton and Company, 1855).

290. Washington, *Maxims* (1855), p. 367.

291. Washington, *Maxims* (1855), p. 367.

292. Washington, *Maxims* (1855), p. 367.

293. Henry Melchoir Muhlenberg, *The Journals of Henry Melchoir Muhlenberg,* Theodore Tappert and John Dobestein, translators (Philadelphia: Evangelical Lutheran Ministerium of Pennsylvania and Adjacent States, 1958), Vol. III, p. 149.

294. *Eulogies and Orations on the Life and Death of General George Washington* (Boston: Manning and Loring, 1800), p. 37, from a eulogy by Jonathan Mitchell Sewall on December 31, 1799.

295. Abiel Holmes, *The Counsel of Washington, Recommended in a Discourse Delivered at Cambridge, February 22, 1800* (Boston: Samuel Hall, 1800), p. 20.

296. *Eulogies* (1800), p. 190, from an oration delivered by Jeremiah Smith on February 22, 1800.

297. Washington, [Sparks] *Writings,* (1838), Vol. XII, pp. 406-407.

298. George Washington, *Maxims of George Washington; Political, Military, Social, Moral, and Religious,* John Frederick Schroeder, editor (Mount Vernon, VA: The Mount Vernon Ladies' Association, 1989).

299. Washington, *Maxims* (1989), p. 164.

300. W. E. Woodward, *George Washington: The Image and the Man* (New York: Boni and Liverlight, 1926), p. 142.

301. Washington, *Writings* (1932), Vol. 15, p. 55, from his speech to the Delaware Indian Chiefs, May 12, 1779.

302. *Facsimile of Manuscript Prayer Book Written by George Washington* (Philadelphia, 1891).

303. Washington, *Writings* (1932), Vol. 5, p. 343, General Orders, July 9, 1776.

304. Washington, *Writings* (1934), Vol. 11, p. 245, General Orders, May 2, 1778.

305. "Washington, D. C. Planned By Masonic Founding Fathers As The Most Powerful Occult Capitol In World History! Part 2," *The Cutting Edge* (at: http://www.cuttingedge.org/news/n1493.cfm) (accessed on August 10, 2010).

306. "In Defence[sic] of satanism," *Jaq D Hawkins* (at: http://jaq.chaosmagic.com/DSatan.htm) (accessed on August 10, 2010).

307. "Everything you always wanted to know about the beliefs of the Founding Fathers that your Congressman will never tell you!" *Real Magick* (at: http://realmagick.com/articles/17/17.html) (accessed on August 10, 2010).

308. "America In Prophecy," *Power of the Cross Ministries* (at: http://www.angelfire.com/nt/books/america.html) (accessed on August 10, 2010).

309. "Freemasonry Source Confirms Our Article News1040 'Masonic Symbols of Power In Their Seat of Power, Washington, D. C.' – That Government Center Was Created in 1792 As A Capitol Dedicated To Masonry," *The Cutting Edge* (at: http://cuttingedge.org/news/n1081.cfm) (accessed on August 10, 2010).

ALSO AVAILABLE FROM WALLBUILDERS

Please go to **www.wallbuilders.com** to view our numerous books, DVDs, CDs, and other resources that will help you rediscover the true history of America's moral, religious, and constitutional heritage.

You may also enjoy browsing through the Historic Documents and Historic Writings section in the "Library" at **www.wallbuilders.com** to see the Founders' own writings!

800-873-2845   ●   WWW.WALLBUILDERS.COM